N A S A / T R E K

NASA/TREK

Popular Science and Sex in America

constance penley

VERSO

E
169.04
P45
1997

First published by Verso in 1997
©Constance Penley
All rights reserved

The right of Constance Penley to be identified as the author of this work
has been asserted by her in accordance with the copyright,
Design and Patents Act 1988.

Verso
UK : 6 Meard Street, London W1V 3HR
USA: 180 Varick Street New York, NY 10014-4606

Verso is the imprint of New Left Books

ISBN 0 86091 617 0 (paper)
ISBN 0 86091 405 4 (cloth)

British Library Cataloguing in Publication Data
A catalogue record is available from the British Library

Library of Congress Cataloging in Publication Data
Penley, Constance, 1948-
    NASA/TREK : popular science and sex in America / Constance Penley.
    p. cm.
    Includes index.
    ISBN 0-86091-405-4 (hc). — ISBN 0-86091-617-0 (pbk.)
    1. Popular culture—United States—History—20th century.
2. Astronautics and civilization. 3. Astronautics in literature.
4. Astronautics in mass media—United States. 5. United States.
National Aeronautics and Space Administration. 6. Star Trek
(Television program) 7. Sex customs—United States—History—20th
century. I. Title.
E169.04.P45 1997
973.91—dc21   97-10902
                                                                CIP

Printed in the USA by R.R. Donnelley & Sons

Book design by Lisa Billard Design, NY

CONTENTS

POPULAR SCIENCE

I grew up in space, enthralled by the sight of rockets taking off from Cape Canaveral. Usually I watched them begin their long arc over the Atlantic from my childhood home in central Florida, only an hour from what came to be called the Kennedy Space Center. But I often got an even closer view of the launches when my father would bundle his sleepy kids into the car to make a pre-dawn dash to the Cape, on little roads through sandy groves and over marshy swamps that I suppose are all paved over now (unless they were lucky enough to be retitled "wetlands"). The coziness and motion of the car usually sent us right back to sleep, but Dad would wake us just in time to glimpse the rocket beginning to roar upwards on its giant plume. Maybe that's why I cannot remember which launches I saw and which ones I dreamed.

My mother made her own contribution to the dreaminess of my space memories by introducing me to the world of science fiction, passing along to me the hundreds of stories and novels she avidly consumed in her "spare time" from work, housekeeping, and raising four kids. The voyages scripted by Asimov, Clarke,

Heinlein, Sturgeon, Bradbury, Ballard, Tiptree, and yes, I am afraid, Hubbard, inextricably wove themselves into my memories of the Pioneer, Gemini, Mercury, and Apollo missions produced by NASA.

Then, at a certain point, I seem to have grown out of space and the fictions of space. I am one of those rare people who cannot remember where they were in 1969 when Neil Armstrong took that first step on the moon, so it must not have made much of an impression on me. I had quit reading science fiction and did not share in the early enthusiasm for *Star Trek*, when it was originally broadcast from 1966 to 1969. I was in college in the late sixties and those were very busy times. Compared to all of my other interests during that period, the space program seemed dangerously frivolous. And who could have known that the clunky little space opera with the bad acting and pointy-eared alien would become, in reruns, such a hugely popular phenomenon and one of the world's largest cultural franchises?

I got back into space and its fictions in the mid-1980s by hanging out with some very interesting women from around the country who write homoerotic, pornographic, utopian romances that take place in the *Star Trek* universe. Fellow academics have insisted that my "hanging out" with these female fan writers was really "doing ethnography," but I cannot bring myself to put that more scholarly grid over the wondrous tangle of experiences and relationships that I found in that fan culture. In the "/TREK" chapter and the ones that follow I talk about everything I learned from this underground group of pseudonymous amateur writers who have ingeniously subverted and rewritten *Star Trek* to make it answerable to their own sexual and social desires. But what I learned most from them was an *attitude* that I later developed into a critical stance, a method of addressing what had become for me the increasingly entwined issues of sex, science, and popular culture. If the "slashers" (as the fans call themselves for reasons that will be revealed later) could rewrite the massive popular phenomenon that is *Star Trek*, why couldn't I rewrite NASA itself? After all, NASA has by now become popular culture—an issue I address in the "NASA/" chapter—making it without doubt an object available to cultural criticism.

The corresponding lesson the fans taught me was that there is no better critic than a fan. No one knows the object better than a fan and no one is more critical. The fan stance toward the object could even be described as the original tough-love approach. The idea is to change the object while preserving it, kind of like giving a strenuous, deep massage that hurts at the time but feels so good afterwards. So I wrote about NASA as a fan of NASA, as a supporter of the scientific, social, and ideological gains of having a space program. All of my criticisms of NASA—and they are myriad, especially concerning its inability to manage the meanings of women in space—are made within a fundamental appreciation of its history and a hope for its future. What I gave up as a critic by adopting the fan method, the righteous rush of the negative critique, I more than gained in the ability to get people to listen to me, which I learned when I was invited to lecture on my NASA research at the Jet Propulsion Laboratory. As I faced my audience, I momentarily panicked in the sudden realization that it is one thing to write *about* NASA and another thing entirely to speak *to* NASA. But even that prickly audience of JPL person-nel relaxed somewhat when I announced at the outset that I was speaking as a fan of NASA. Once they knew that I was there not as a harsh detractor or glib debunker, they were able to take in my criticisms, no matter how scathing, enunciated as they were within an overall appreciation of NASA.

Finally, the fans taught me the value of boldly going where no one has gone before. Rewrite NASA?! Sure. On the face of it, that sounds like a delusional, overreaching, arrogant, and ridicu-lously utopian ambition. But what if that rewriting is already going on, and all I am doing is making that project visible and then joining in? Rewriting *Star Trek* and rewriting NASA—rewriting the blended cultural text I later call "NASA/TREK"—are both part of a large, ongoing popular engagement with issues of science and technology.

Science is popular in America. An astonishing number of ordinary Americans take an extraordinary interest in exploring the human relation to science and technology. In turn, the insti-tutions of science and technology increasingly strive to be popu-lar, that is, to try to find ways to communicate their ideas and endeavors in such a way that people (in government, the media, and everyday life) feel they are sufficiently part of those ideas and endeavors to want to lend their enthusiastic support. *NASA/TREK* sketches a picture of our collective, if sometimes conflictual, imaginary of that human relation to science and tech-nology. I start with the claim that "going into space"—both the actuality of it and its science fiction realization—has become the prime metaphor through which we try to make sense of the world of science and technology and imagine a place for ourselves in it. The yearning to get a personal grip on that seemingly distant realm can be seen everywhere in American popular culture and everyday life, if one only knows how to recognize it and, at least provisionally, accept it on its own terms.

Recognizing and accepting this popular will to do science does not come easy, especially when "the experts" start from the assumption that most citizens are shamefully ignorant of scientific issues. Take, for example, the position of America's most famous science popularizer, astronomer and space scientist Carl Sagan. In *The Demon-Haunted World: Science as a Candle in the Dark*, the most recent of many books in which Sagan attempts to describe and explain scientific ideas and methods to nonscientists, he decries the distortions of science promoted by a popular culture that robs people of their skepticism and leaves them vulnerable to the appeal of pseudoscience and even antiscience.[1] Sagan believes that *Star Trek*, for example, dupes viewers into scientific ignorance by eschewing the most elementary scientific facts, as seen in the idea that "Mr. Spock could be a cross between a human being and a life-form independently evolved on the planet Vulcan" (375). Genetically, he says, this is far less probable than a successful cross of a man and an artichoke. *The X-Files*, too, comes in for Sagan's special ire for paying "lipservice" to skeptical examination of the paranormal but skewing heavily toward the reality of alien abductions and government coverups of anything strange or interesting (374). Entertainment, for Sagan, is the opposite of enlightenment; popular science and science cannot coexist because popular science ("irrationality") confounds the progress of science ("rationality").

Such a view contrasts sharply with that of another famous scientist who has also successfully popularized space science, physicist Stephen Hawking. Hawking made a memorable appearance on *Star Trek: The Next Generation*, in which, at the invitation of his cyborg counterpart, Data, he joined a hologram Newton and Einstein for a game of poker and a gab about physics aboard the *Enterprise*. And when Hawking introduced fellow physicist Lawrence Krauss's *The Physics of Star Trek*, he focused not so much on *Star Trek*'s physics bloopers (which Krauss hilariously covers with his top ten list selected by Nobel Prize–winning physicists and NASA scientists) but, more importantly, on the ways in which fans can use *Star Trek* to think about scientific ideas such as the nature of time and energy. For Hawking, an engagement with popular science, here the fictional *Star Trek* universe, enables a rational understanding of the universe.

Sagan, on the other hand, believes that people have a natural appetite for science but that "spurious" popular culture accounts "snare the gullible"(5), attracting them to "the cheap imitation" instead of "real science"(4). We are "naive," "mislead," "bamboozled," he says, like the cab driver whose exchange with Sagan opens the book. On the way from the airport to a conference of scientists and TV broadcasters devoted to "the seemingly hopeless prospect of improving the presentation of science on commercial television," the cab driver asks whether the famous scientist would be willing to answer some of his questions about science. Given the go-ahead, the cabby discusses in great detail the alien corpses in that Air Force hanger, the prophecies of

Nostradamus, the shroud of Turin, and the underwater expeditions to find the ruins of Atlantis. Sagan describes the cab driver's initial "buoyant enthusiasm" and then his turning "glummer and glummer" as the scientist pours ever-more cold water on that enthusiasm by insisting that there is no evidence for any of these ideas. Sagan acknowledges, "I was dismissing not just some errant doctrine, but a precious facet of his inner life"(4). But he does not seem to recognize that "precious facet" as what he earlier called the natural appetite for science. For Sagan, the only way lay people can extend their natural appetite is to follow scientists like himself, the bearers of the candle in the dark. Our pleasure in science, he insists, should emerge only through identification with the righteous joy of *his* skeptical debunking of nonscience.

No one would ever take Sagan for a populist, especially after the way he uses the cabby's enthusiasm as a vehicle to deplore widespread scientific illiteracy and mindless adherence to popular accounts of science. (In my reading of the exchange, by the way, the cab driver was having him on.) But Sagan's total dismissal of all popular engagement with the world of science and technology, except insofar as that engagement can be channeled through scientist-professionals like himself, means that so much of the popular investment in science and technology that I want to show is the warp and woof of American culture remains invisible, and socially unaccounted for.

Sagan's first problem is that he simply misreads texts. *The X-Files*, for example, does not try to substitute spiritualism for science nor does it eschew skepticism. Instead, the show uses that which has been declared outside the bounds of science to challenge the categories and methods of science. It is fully skeptical, but its skepticism is turned toward the complicity of establishment science and the government in resisting people who believe that science is too important to be left to the scientists.[2] Sagan also misses the humor of *The X-Files* and how that humor is used to mock the pretensions and secretiveness of scientific-government institutions. In my favorite episode, agents Scully and Mulder discover why the *Challenger* blew up, the *Mars Observer* disappeared, *Galileo*'s antenna got stuck, and the *Hubble*'s lenses were misground: they were all sabotaged by a former astronaut, now a high-up bureaucrat at NASA, whose body was taken over by an alien on one of the late sixties space flights. Why are aliens sabotaging every NASA attempt to go into space? "They" don't want us out there, of course—it's theirs! *The X-Files* taunt to NASA seems to be, "If you keep on covering up or downplaying your mistakes, we'll create our own ingenious reasons for this sorry record." Or, "Our fictional alibi (the aliens did it) to account for all the NASA screw-ups is no more outrageous than the excuses you've contrived."

If Sagan cannot appreciate the levels of irony and humor in *The X-Files*, he certainly would not be able to recognize what fans of *The X-Files* are doing with the show. They catch all of the show's subtly intelligent fun with science (see the Internet chat groups and the fan literature spinning off from the show) and especially enjoy *The X-Files'* undermining of sexual stereotypes. The female Scully is rational, skeptical, and devoted to conventional scientific method, in contrast to her male partner's emotionality, attraction to the supernatural, and total lack of scientific superego.

Perhaps Sagan would be able to recognize the degree of critical reflection fans are capable of if he would only extend to them the same credit he clearly gives to participants in his own fan culture. As cofounder and president of the Planetary Society, the largest space interest group in the world, Sagan is active in promoting involvement in both space science and space policy. The space fans who make up the Planetary Society membership (and who presumably have to check any popular culture allegiances at the clubhouse door) are engaging in behavior that is really no different from Trekkers, X-philes, NASA-garbed technoravers, and even the tabloiders (ROSS PEROT IS AN ALIEN! NASA FINDS FACE ON MARS!). They all want to get a human grip on the world of science and technology, a project whose most compelling metaphor or script is that of going into space. And they all want to have a say about who will be able to go there, despite the efforts of humorless, antipopulist gatekeepers like Sagan. If it seems that I am picking on Sagan, it is only because he is the most well-known science popularizer, and thus the most familiar example I could cite. But it is also because he has become so doggedly vehement in his denunciations of popular culture and people's everyday engagement with science and technology.

NASA/TREK, as I will describe it, is popular science. It is a collectively elaborated story that weaves together science and science fiction to help write, think, and launch us into space. Popular science involves the efforts of scientists, science writers, and scientific institutions to attract interest and support for advancing science and technology. Popular science includes the many science fiction television shows (and fewer films) that offer a personalized, utopian reflection on men and women in space. Popular science is fictional work that carries on this reflection. Popular science is ordinary people's extraordinary will to engage with the world of science and technology. Popular science wants us to go into space but keep our feet on the ground. Popular science envisions a science that boldly goes where no one has gone before but remains answerable to human needs and social desires. Popular science, fully in the American utopian tradition, proposes that scientific experimentation be accompanied by social and sexual experimentation. Popular science insists that we are, or should be, popular scientists one and all.

NASA /

Just as the phrase "rocket scientist" remains everyday parlance for someone who is both brainy and butch, the acronym "NASA" serves as a popular reference for individual ingenuity and collective can-do. A community activist in South Central Los Angeles says the gang problem can be solved but it will take the kind of effort it took NASA to get a man on the moon. A chef in New York distinguishes his restaurant from another by describing the rival cooks as very rah-rah masculine, whereas his own are like NASA technicians who just come in and get the job done. A cultural entrepreneur on the East Coast mounts ecstatic weekly technoraves under the name NASA—Nocturnal Audio Sensory Awakening. The hero of Kidlat Tahimik's film *The Perfumed Nightmare* (1978) energizes the kids in his destitute Philippine village by getting them to band together in a Wernher von Braun fan club (with all irony about the kids' adulation for a Nazi turned NASA scientist intended). Even with NASA's myriad known failings—not to mention the ones it covers up—the space agency continues to represent, however improbably, creativity, cooperation, and perseverance. NASA's polysemous meanings can still be mobilized to rejuvenate the near-moribund idea of an ideal future toward which dedicated people could work.

But it takes a lot of doing. To keep those meanings mobilized NASA seems to have adopted the film industry's summer blockbuster approach. During the summer of 1994, the twenty-fifth anniversary of the *Apollo 11* moon landing, former astronaut Buzz Aldrin was everywhere, talking about the mission (but Alan Shepard beat him to the Home Shopping Network). Although the first man on the moon, the modest and self-effacing Neil Armstrong, resisted serving as NASA's poster boy for manned spaceflight, there were innumerable books, journalistic retrospectives, videos, and television specials that endlessly replayed NASA's most glorious triumph. But clearly this celebration was shot through with nostalgia for what may never be again.

The following summer it was director Ron Howard's turn to evoke those heady times, and he did so spectacularly with the blockbuster film *Apollo 13*. Ironically, though, *Apollo 13* was able to showcase NASA's best qualities only by reproducing the agency during its most severe crisis. Using only duct tape and gumption, NASA teamwork turned doom into deliverance, saving the lives of three stranded astronauts, not to mention the future of the entire Apollo program. By heroicizing the astronauts and the Mission Control team that saved them, the film inadvertently suggests what NASA critics have said all along: the space agency is good at crisis management but lacks a strategic vision, the kind of conceptualizing that goes into long-term planning and effective communication of its mission to the public. But at least *Apollo 13* believes in NASA as a crucial site of utopian ideas and yearnings.

The utopic image of NASA shown in *Apollo 13* was a far cry from that seen in *Capricorn One*, a 1978 film that depicts an agency so underfunded yet bloated, so chaotic and incompetent that it has to fake a Mars landing in a movie studio, knowing it does not have the resources and technology to pull off the real thing but desperately needing the spectacle of a successful mission to regain popular support and federal funding. Ron Howard's film, by contrast, recreates an era when NASA appeared faultless and heroic, even though its usefulness as one of the main ideological weapons in the Cold War was rapidly ebbing.

Whether NASA could still translate utopian idealism into scientific accomplishment was the question at the center of much of the media coverage of *Apollo 13*. Critics were sharply divided over the role the film would play in garnering public support for future space science and exploration, particularly at a time when congressional budget cuts were defunding research, education, and environmental programs. Some felt that the film's reminder of NASA's glory days and the poignant concluding words — when Tom Hanks, America's most popular actor ruminates, "I wonder if we'll ever go back there and I wonder who they will be?" — would renew public interest and support for the space program. This is clearly what the White House had in mind when it invited Hanks to a Capitol Hill reception just days before a House debate over funding for the space station. In his real-life role Hanks insisted that he was not lobbying for NASA but nevertheless made a pitch for the space station, saying "I would like to be able to stand out in my backyard one night with my kids and look up at the space station *Freedom* as it goes by." A nearby White House official winked and called Hanks "our secret weapon." And indeed the ploy seems to have worked since the House subsequently defeated two straight attempts to kill the space station—the last one by the widest victory margin in years.[3]

More skeptical critics of the film, however, saw *Apollo 13* as simple nostalgia-mongering, pitched to a public that loves the retro chic value of the seventies, but has no real interest in furthering scientific discovery. These critics pointed out that while audiences were thronging to *Apollo 13* hardly anyone was paying attention to the real action going on in real space, the historic docking of the American space shuttle *Atlantis* and the Russian space station *Mir*. People these days, the critics concluded, prefer their reality digitized and imagineered.

The cynical reception of *Apollo 13* demonstrated that despite the public's enthusiasm for the space heroics of Tom Hanks, NASA's ability to serve as a utopian referent has considerably weakened. In fact, it is astonishing that NASA can generate any positive spin at all, since one lingering effect of *Apollo 13* was to remind viewers that when NASA fails, it does so spectacularly. And there is not always a nice, heroic save as with the *Apollo 13* debacle. The reality of NASA's past record is more disastrous: the 1967 *Apollo* fire that killed three astronauts on the launchpad, the disappearance of the *Mars Observer*, the faulty *Hubble* lens, *Galileo's* stuck antenna and broken tape recorder, and of course the *Challenger* explosion. The credibility of NASA has also been damaged by its own bombast and broken promises, the fraudulent billing and shoddy work of its corporate contractors, the dramatic aging of its work force, its laughably out-of-date technology, and an awkward and inefficient bureaucracy.

Thus NASA's summer blockbuster for 1996 was a sort of hail-Mary pass: the startling announcement that NASA scientists had found the first real proof of life on Mars. President Clinton called the discovery "one of the most stunning insights into our universe that science has ever uncovered." And of course, NASA Chief Daniel Goldin immediately exploited the event to campaign for resuscitating the budget-doomed Mission to Mars. But skeptics worried that NASA had once again released premature and hyperbolic conclusions and that this hasty political deployment of merely suggestive findings might result in the biggest scientific embarrassment since the initial (and erroneous) reports of cold fusion seven years before. (Meanwhile, *Independence Day*, the blockbuster film of summer 1996, simply mocked the hapless space agency's anachronistic right-stuff image: the hero fighter pilot who saves the world from alien invasion dreams of being an astronaut but, as one of his buddies reminds him, NASA would never accept an astronaut whose fiancée is a stripper.)

Why, then, does NASA remain a repository for utopian meanings? Obviously public attitudes toward NASA are not based solely on scientific achievement or political spin control. We process our knowledge of NASA in a variety of more or less unconscious ways, ranging from simple displacement to outright denial. A lot of this individual and collective refashioning of NASA's meanings tends to be wish-fulfilling, to produce the NASA we want, not the one we have. And here the stuffy space agency is aided (again, more or less unconsciously) by an increasing symbolic merging with its hugely popular fictional twin, *Star Trek*. Together they form a powerful cultural icon, a force that I call "NASA/TREK." This new entity NASA/TREK shapes our popular and institutional imaginings about space exploration by humanizing our relation to science and technology. It also gives us a language to describe and explain the world and to express yearnings for a different and better condition; it is, then, a common language for utopia.

How did this improbable symbolic merging occur? What kind of new story about the world of space (and this world) does the NASA/TREK narrative tell? What controls this mutated semi-fictional space saga? If it omits or distorts certain important ideas, can it be rewritten? And, if so, by whom? To begin to answer some of these questions, it is useful to consider some of the characteristics of *Star Trek* that make its symbolic union with NASA so plausible. *Star Trek* began as a television show, originally broadcast from 1966 to 1969, now referred to by fans as "classic" Trek. But since then it has grown into a vast popular culture empire, including television spinoffs (*Star Trek: The Next Generation*, *Deep Space Nine*, and *Star Trek: Voyager*), eight movies, hundreds of best-selling novels, video games, action figures, fan conventions, fan amateur publications ("zines"), and now even its own television network — UPN. Little needs to be said about the ubiquity of Trek lore and language: you cannot get through a day without seeing, hearing, or reading a reference to *Star Trek*, no matter what your job or social milieu. The fictional and fan world of *Star Trek* has been called a religion, a cult, and the most elaborate alternate universe ever created. It is a new form of global village in which the citizens engage in an ongoing conversation on what it means to be human in a technological and multicultural world.[4]

For better or for worse, an astonishingly complex popular discourse about civic, social, moral, and political issues is filtered through the idiom and ideas of *Star Trek*. Here are just a few random examples: a newspaper editorial wonders plaintively why the Defense Department cannot be less *Star Wars* and more *Star Trek*; the Pentagon invokes the image of Captain Kirk saying "Set your phasers on stun" to sway legislators to fund "nonlethal" weapons (they are actually "prelethal" weapons that immobilize the enemy prior to killing him); a couple on a primetime sitcom decides not to interfere in the problems of a younger couple because of *Star Trek*'s Prime Directive, a Federation rule against interference in developing cultures — but then they do intervene after acknowledging that the Prime Directive was constantly broken on *Star Trek*! Elsewhere, Brooklyn TQs ("teen queens" who have run away from home to live in crack houses) deploy the language of *Star Trek* as they go on "missions" to raise money, dubbing crack "Scotty" and getting high "beaming up." In Los Angeles, the friends of a white man killed by blacks in the uprising following the Rodney King beating verdicts call his death ironic, saying that he was a staunch anti racist because he was a Trekker who lived by the Vulcan precept of IDIC ("Infinite Diversity in Infinitive Combinations"). In its annual "Women We Love" issue, *Esquire* magazine celebrates Barbara Adams, an alternate Whitewater trial juror who reported for duty in full *Star Trek* uniform, complete with tricorder and phaser. (Adams, the head of a local "ship," or chapter, of the Federation alliance, a

Star Trek fan group, said she wore the outfit to court to promote the program's "ideas, messages and good solid values.") Then there are the myriad *Star Trek* bumper stickers: "Beam me up Scotty, there's no intelligent life here," "Beam me up, Lord" (the Christian version), or "Picard and Riker in '92" (for the politically inclined). Best-selling authors have also learned the efficacy of communicating their ideas through *Star Trek*; their works range from the very useful *The Physics of Star Trek* by Lawrence M. Krauss to the lame *Make It So: Leadership Lessons from Star Trek: The Next Generation* by Wess Roberts (author of *Leadership Secrets of Attila the Hun*) and Bill Ross.

But less noted than the extent to which vignettes of *Star Trek* pervade our everyday lives is the way that NASA and *Star Trek* have merged. For one thing, people who work for NASA are about as Trekked-out as people anywhere, perhaps in part because Trek lore and language lends itself well to a work culture devoted to the science and technology of space exploration. Mission Control computers have been called Scotty and Uhura and the shuttle's on-board computer is named—what else?— Spock. The working name of the proposed sequel to the Hubble Space Telescope is "Space Telescope Next Generation." And many of the astronauts have been vocal about the inspiration they received from *Star Trek*. Mae Jemison, the first African-American woman in space, says that it was Nichelle Nichols in her role as Lt. Uhura, the African communications officer on board the *Enterprise*, who made her first want to go into space.

But at an even more fundamental institutional level, NASA has deliberately participated in making itself over as *Star Trek*, or at least has welcomed internal and external pressure to do so. NASA first began its *Star Trek* makeover in the mid-seventies when the space agency yielded to President Gerald Ford's demand (prompted by a *Star Trek* fan letter-writing campaign) to change the name of the first shuttle from *Constitution* to *Enterprise*. Many of the show's cast members were there as the *Enterprise*—an experimental model used only to practice takeoff and landing—was rolled out onto the tarmac at Edwards Air Force Base to the stirring sounds of Alexander Courage's theme from *Star Trek*. After *Star Trek* creator Gene Roddenberry died in 1991, NASA let an unnamed shuttle astronaut carry his ashes—classified as "personal effects"—into space. And NASA actually hired Nichelle Nichols at one point in the late seventies to help recruit women and minorities into the astronaut corps. Mae Jemison later invited Nichols to her launch and began every shift of her shuttle mission with Lt. Uhura's famous line, "Hailing frequencies open."[5] Even the Smithsonian's National Air and Space Museum, which produces and houses the historical record of U.S. space flight, has made a point of including *Star Trek*. In March 1992 the museum mounted *Star Trek: The Exhibition*, a show that turned out to be wildly popular (big surprise). In response to the question of what a pop-culture phenomenon like *Star Trek* was doing in a place that honors real-life conquests of air and space, the curator said, simply, "There is no other fantasy more pervasive in the conceptualization of space flight than *Star Trek*."[6] One might conclude from these examples that *Star Trek* is the theory, NASA the practice.

But the intertextual references do not just go one way. The

first *Star Trek* film, Robert Wise's *Star Trek: The Motion Picture* (1979), concerns an encounter between the *Enterprise* and a large, sentient machine-planet that is charging toward Earth to find its "creator," not realizing that it is so large that its presence in the solar system will destroy Earth. The crew discover—just in time to save Earth!—that the heart of this machine-planet is *Voyager*, one of two tiny satellites sent out by NASA in 1977, now returning from interstellar space with alien encrustations and its own developed intelligence. A sequel, *Star Trek IV: The Voyage Home* (1986), was dedicated to the martyred astronauts of the space shuttle *Challenger*. And one of the shuttlecraft on *Star Trek: The Next Generation* was named *Onizuka* after Ellison Onizuka of the *Challenger* crew. When Mae Jemison retired from NASA, she did a cameo as a transporter officer on an episode of *The Next Generation*.

Why would a button-down agency like NASA want to take on the trappings of a popular phenomenon like *Star Trek*? (Or, for that matter, vice versa?) To ask this question is to ask whether NASA should itself aim *to be* popular culture. Literary theorist Fredric Jameson points out that American science fiction generally shows an affinity for dystopian rather than utopian futures, often featuring fantasies of cyclical regression or totalitarian empires. Our love affair with apocalypse and Armageddon, he says, results from a degeneration of the utopian imagination. If *Star Trek* stands out as a rare utopian scenario of our scientific and technological future, it makes perfect sense that NASA would want to align itself with that hugely popular story of things to come.

For another thing, the fate of the space station most likely depends on its supporters' ability to ensure that future through successfully weaving the need for such a facility into the NASA/TREK scenario (along with, of course, a great deal of baldfaced porkbarrelling by legislators from Southern California and the Houston area, where the components will be built). Even some of the harshest critics of the space station believe its construction should be supported insofar as it would contribute to a new era of international cooperation, especially with the former Evil Empire. Ironically, the original *Star Trek* series implied such cooperation had already been achieved by including (controversially in 1966) a Russian from a peaceful Earth among its crew. More practical considerations are also relevant, such as the desire to stabilize the Soviet aerospace industry to lessen its temptation to sell dangerous technology to other countries. But the ideological and utopian considerations are important too: the world could use an orbiting icon symbolizing the peaceful collaboration of old enemies—especially since we know that icons do not just "symbolize" but have their own determining effects on social reality.

The answer to the question about whether NASA should be trafficking in the popular, then, depends on the job it seems to be doing of writing its own script. A look at one of NASA's biggest public relations stunts, the Teacher in Space program, shows just how badly the agency has botched that script in the past. Ideally, by examining this extreme instance of NASA's failure to be popular we can begin to understand the kind of work—historical, empirical, political, cultural—that would be necessary for any possible rewrite in the future.

SPACED OUT

The first sick joke I heard about the *Challenger* explosion was:
What were Christa McAuliffe's last words?
"Hey, guys, what's this button?"

The second one was:
What's a *Challenger* Cocktail?
7-Up and a splash of Teachers.

And then, equally to the point:
Where did Christa McAuliffe spend her vacation?
All up and down the Florida coast.

NASA's mismanagement of the life and death of Christa McAuliffe reproduced and reinvigorated several pernicious cultural narratives about women in space. These myths are gruesomely apparent in the sick jokes that sprang up after the *Challenger* disaster.[7] If we accept that "space" remains one of the major sites of utopian thinking and that "going into space" is still one of the most important ways we represent our relation to science, technology, and the future, we need to examine the stories we tell ourselves about space and about women in space. We would then be able to ask how and by whom those stories could be rewritten, in part so that they do not block women from being part of the world of "space" or perversely account for them once they are there. When I say "women in space," I also mean to include not only female astronauts but also their more earthbound counterparts, such as female scientists and engineers (at NASA and elsewhere), as well as women with strong space interests like Senator Barbara A. Mikulski (D-Md.), who heads the important subcommittee that oversees NASA's budget.

"HEY, GUYS, WHAT'S THIS BUTTON?"

Let's consider the first joke, the one with the punchline "Hey, guys, what's this button?" In this version of the woman in space, McAuliffe is the vamp in the machine, the female wrench in the works, joining a long line of radioactive and exploding women in science fiction film, and repeating the frequent conflation of women-out-of-control with technology-out-of-control.[8] McAuliffe reported that, during training, she was told "in serious jest" by Commander Dick Scobee never to touch any of the thirteen hundred switches in the shuttle cockpit simulator. In the joke version — a variant on the moron joke — catastrophe is seen to ensue because the woman is stupid, ill-qualified, or out of place. The basis of this joke is the belief that McAuliffe should never have been part of the *Challenger* crew in the first place, a belief which is, I think, correct.

The Teacher in Space program — strongly opposed by U.S. education leaders — was a Reagan-Bush-NASA media circus. The selection committee included Pam Dawber, whose closest link to space science was her TV role as the earthbound girlfriend of the wacky alien Mork on *Mork and Mindy*, and the ceremony for the finalists looked like a cross between the Academy Awards and the Miss America Pageant. McAuliffe, who charmingly explained that "all I really knew about space travel before [meeting my first astronaut] was what I'd seen on *Star Trek*," was undeniably eager and enthusiastic about her mission to space. But even Robert T. Hohler, her respectful and sympathetic biographer, noted that "Christa was not the brightest of the ten finalists," a group that included a prize-winning playwright and poet, several multilingual world travelers, a former fighter pilot, a film producer, and a union organizer.[9] A blurb on the back cover of his biography says, "It will take a heart of stone to read *I Touch the Future*...without shedding more tears over the fate of Christa McAuliffe." Readers will indeed shed tears over McAuliffe's brave martyrdom, but some of those readers may cry instead over the discovery that she was selected for her representative mediocrity *and knew it*.

Make no mistake: the point here is not to fault McAuliffe for her lack of skills or knowledge or to fault NASA for attempting to be popular. Rather, the issue is why the Teacher in Space scheme was so wrongly conceived and disastrously executed. What didn't we see then what we can understand now? What can we do so that Christa McAuliffe will not remain lost in space? She was a teacher, and we should still be able to learn from her. The lessons we take, however, may not be the official ones.

In NASA's view, McAuliffe was perfect, the all-American girl next door: pretty but not too pretty, competent but no intellectual, a traditional mother and teacher whose lawyer husband was her high school sweetheart. She led a Girl Scout troop, volunteered all over town, and taught catechism. Hohler's biography reports that during the months of training at the Johnson Space

Center McAuliffe spent her spare time reading *Good Housekeeping*, working on her needlepoint, and baking apple pies. McAuliffe also passed the FBI background check, which included, among many other things, asking her husband whether she had ever had any affairs. She exemplified what Elaine Tyler May has called "the American tradition of Republican motherhood." In her study of Cold War–era symbols linking masculine fears of atomic power, sex, and women out of control, May notes (following Linda Kerber) that ever since the Revolution, American political ideology has held a special place for women as the nurturers and educators of future citizens. During the Cold War, May says, women were the symbolic linchpin in the development of civil defense strategies to "tame fears of the atomic age by linking survival and security to traditional family values." McAuliffe also functioned to domesticate NASA in much the same way that women in factories in nineteenth-century America were expected to tame the ravages of industrial capitalism with their feminine purity and order.[10]

McAuliffe's only perceived drawback as a symbolic astronaut candidate was her zeal for citing John F. Kennedy's ideas on citizenship as the major influence on her life and career. From the Nixon administration on, Republicans had been trying to distance NASA's achievements from Kennedy's own popularity. For twenty years, Kennedy's tremendous personal support for the manned space program had stood in marked contrast to later Republican indifference, that is, until the mid-1980s when Ronald Reagan perceived the shuttle's uses for deploying Star Wars components. After McAuliffe began giving interviews,

James M. Beggs, the head of NASA who had originally suggested sending a teacher into space, got a call from the Reagan White House: "Deaver told me to tell her not to talk." Beggs passed Deaver's warning on to McAuliffe, who then contained her expressions of admiration for Kennedy." NASA had already infuriated the Reagan White House by inviting former antiwar activist Jane Fonda to attend the launch of Sally Ride, the first American woman in space.

Unfortunately, NASA's eagerness to choose the citizen with the best symbolic capital to play the role of teacher-as-all-American-hero created problems that the agency never addressed, either at the time or after the catastrophic failure of the project. For example, every teacher-finalist was to propose a project that he or she would carry out during the mission. Most of the proposals involved demonstrations of scientific principles. But McAuliffe, with no science background, simply proposed to keep a journal of her experiences during training, flight, and afterwards. In her application she compared herself to the women pioneers who traveled across the plains in Conestoga wagons, keeping personal journals of their experiences and writing letters back East. After her death it was found that she had made almost no journal entries during her months of training.

Moreover, the biography tells us, "science baffled her." At one point, her NASA educational coordinator almost quit over McAuliffe's resistance to learning even the most basic scientific principles needed to demonstrate the effects of weightlessness on plant growth, simple machines, effervescence, magnetism, chromatography, and Newton's laws of gravity. Ultimately, McAuliffe mastered the demonstrations, but only after her instructor had greatly simplified them to suit her limited science skills. Even *Challenger* (ABC,1989), the cloying and celebratory made-for-TV movie, harped on McAuliffe's lack of math abilities and her resistance to science. In the movie, this deficiency is "resolved" by showing her improving at math. Commander Dick Scobee throws simple multiplication questions at her, and she invariably gets them wrong. But she gradually goes from being only 10 percent off to only 2 percent off. "Good enough for a teacher," he cracks. Christa's learning curve increases as she slowly comes to appreciate the beauty and importance of the science lessons she is expected to present from space.[12]

Several sick jokes about McAuliffe in the *Challenger* joke cycle capitalize on the image of an inept female teacher:

> What was the last thing that went through Christa McAuliffe's head?
> A piece of the fuselage.

or:

> How do you get rid of a teacher?
> Challenge her.

or this variant:

> I can't believe it. Seven months of training and she still went to pieces after takeoff.[13]

These jokes illustrate just how unfortunate it was that NASA chose a teacher who could be so easily caricatured as the dumb, poorly trained teacher then being scapegoated by conservatives for the failure of the American public school system.

When folklorist Patrick D. Morrow collected and analyzed many of the sick jokes that began to circulate after the *Challenger* disaster, he found that most of them centered on Christa McAuliffe.[14] Borrowing Freud's description of the dynamic of the joke, he argued that the *Challenger* jokes matched the requirement that three persons be involved: the one making the joke, the one who is the object of hostility or sexual aggression, and the one for whom the joke is supposed to produce pleasure. In his article, Morrow admits that McAuliffe is the apparent butt of most of these jokes but he claims that the real target is the "depersonalized and inhuman forces that killed her." We don't objectify McAuliffe, he believes, we identify with her; she is the woman civilian and amateur astronaut who, like other ordinary people, is prone to error. Moreover, she is the victim, the one who was killed, "Who would want to attack her?" (181). According to Morrow, the jokes are culturally significant as a subversive popular critique of the "technological powers-that-be"—not spelled out by Morrow—and he celebrates the jokes as such.

Film theorist Patricia Mellencamp offers an elegant and persuasive rebuttal to Morrow's interpretation of these sick jokes, citing the part of Freud's description of the three-party joke that Morrow leaves out: the blame that invariably gets ascribed to the woman when she is one of the three parties.[15] Mellencamp shows how the jokes, which target McAuliffe's amateurism, turn the disastrous mission into a wacky episode of *I Love Lucy* with the teacher as a kind of space-age Lucy Ricardo. "Women, as leftovers or aftereffects, become the objects of jokes or malicious gossip, their asserted subjectivity the real target, analyzed as with Lucy, as lack of ability" (258). Although these jokes offer some elements of a popular criticism of NASA's bad judgment in choosing, for example, to send into space a nonprofessional with limited scientific abilities, Mellencamp is right to detect here another popular discourse, a story of women's inherent deficiencies, which become glaringly visible—and risible—whenever she forgets her place.

The situation was no smoother for highly trained, professional female astronauts. Electrical engineer and mission specialist Judith Resnick, the other woman who flew on *Challenger*, had her own difficulties with the symbolic meanings insistently imposed on her. Because of her tough intelligence, even her friends called her "J.R." But Resnick bristled when people called her "the second woman in space" (after Sally Ride) or "the first Jewish astronaut." In interviews she would say, "I am an astronaut. Not a woman astronaut. Not a Jewish astronaut. An astronaut."

In McAuliffe's case, the media hook was precisely her representative mediocrity, which was immediately given a more appealing spin as her "ordinariness." (The makers of the animated comedy *The Simpsons* later mocked this ideological move in an episode in which the decidedly lowbrow Homer Simpson is picked to be an astronaut.) NASA hoped the public would re-identify with the agency and its costly projects through identification with McAuliffe in her role as ordinary wife, mother, teacher, and private citizen in space. And the media, with the right nudges from NASA, hopped on the largest public-relations bandwagon ever mobilized by the space agency. McAuliffe had to bear a huge representational load: on her shoulders rested the hopes for public support of U.S. space exploration at a time when its future looked particularly precarious.[16]

Since the early 1980s the Reagan White House had been insisting that the shuttle should be used to ferry Star Wars components and spy satellites into orbit, with crew members drawn from a secret military astronaut corps. For its part, the military had no interest in using a space vehicle operated by low-security civilians. When invited to provide its design requirements, the Pentagon asked for so many augmentations that if they had all been made the shuttle would never have gotten off the ground. In fact, the military hoped to go back to lofting their military wares into space on unmanned rockets. But meanwhile, private companies with loads scheduled to be launched were complaining loudly about the delays and Congress was looking to make budget cuts in the notoriously porkbarrelled space program. And NASA had literally lost its head. In 1985 Chief Administrator James Beggs was forced to take an unexpected leave of absence to fight charges that he had defrauded the Department of Defense several years earlier while he was an executive vice-president of General Dynamics Corporation. The acting chief administrator, Bill Graham, was politicking on Capitol Hill at the time of the *Challenger* launch.

In *The Final Frontier*, Dale Carter says the Reagan White House and NASA conceived of the *Challenger* mission in this way:

Where the orbiter was a powerful and majestic product of daring scientific ability, free enterprise innovation, and bold political leadership which had risen like a patriotic phoenix from the ashes of a generation's military defeat, social disorder, and administrative corruption, Christa McAuliffe was a figure of talent, personal initiative, and commitment whose hard work and sacrifice during that era of American stagnation had given rise to individual achievement and satisfaction. Where the orbiter was the harbinger of a high technology revolution that would bring prosperity and stability to enterprising Americans, Christa McAuliffe was an example of the well-educated middle-class professional whose role would be to introduce the citizens of the future to the vistas of space age opportunity facilitated by science, mathematics, and individual excellence. (256-257)

At least that was the idea.

NASA denied that McAuliffe's selection was in any way political. But, in addition to being a woman, she was from New Hampshire, the site of the nation's first presidential primary—a possible benefit to Vice President Bush's upcoming 1992 presidential campaign—and a state whose school system did well with minimal federal aid, a point of pride for President Reagan. NASA also denied that the *Challenger* launch time was a political decision, though the Reagan staff had lobbied for the shuttle mission to coincide with the president's January 1986 State of the Union address, during which he hoped to talk directly to the teacher in space.[17] On the other hand, Kitty Kelley's biography of Nancy Reagan says it was Ronald Reagan's personal White House astrologer who suggested the most propitious launch time.[18]

"7-UP AND A SPLASH OF TEACHERS"

The horror of women in space that echoes in this line is the horror of what has become a collective public disavowal. Christa McAuliffe and the other six astronauts on the *Challenger* did not die when it exploded, as most people imagine, but when it splashed down. The crew cabin was intact; it was blasted free from the fuselage and continued on its upward trajectory for twenty-five seconds before descending to hit the ocean almost three minutes later. Some individual airpacks had been turned on manually, including one (later identified as belonging to Pilot Mike Smith) that was found to have three-fourths to seven-eighths of its six-minute supply depleted.[19] Under the Freedom of Information Act, *Time*, the *New York Times*, and the *Journal of the American Medical Association* have tried to get audiotapes of the *Challenger*'s final moments and autopsy reports on the recovered bodies. But NASA has steadfastly refused both requests in the name of protecting the privacy of the astronauts' families.[20] More likely, NASA administrators fear that public knowledge of how the astronauts died would increase the horror of the event.

But NASA apparently also worried that such disclosures would increase demands for costly safety mechanisms at a time when NASA had little credibility to ask for more money. Surely Congress—and future astronauts—would demand an in-flight emergency escape system if it were proven that the *Challenger* astronauts could have survived with one. Although the *Mercury*, *Gemini*, and *Apollo* spacecrafts all had escape systems, one was never developed for the space shuttle because of NASA's shortsighted belt-tightening. In the original proposal for the space shuttle NASA presented a budget that it knew was inadequate but that it thought could squeak by Congress. (The same strategy enabled congressional approval of the space station in 1993.) Nor was this the first time NASA thought it could gain through a coverup. After a launchpad fire killed three *Apollo* astronauts in 1967, NASA had falsely maintained that Roger Chaffee, Virgil Grissom, and Edward White had died instantly in the fire. Senator Walter Mondale became the agency's sharpest watchdog and severest foe when documents leaked to him revealed that hundreds of NASA staff members had heard the astronauts' minutes-long screams of agony over an open-voice circuit that had been preserved on tape.

Our knowing and not knowing how Christa McAuliffe and the other *Challenger* astronauts died—the disavowal echoed in the gagline "7-Up and a splash of Teachers"—opens up a symbolic void to be filled with our own worst imaginings. Perhaps the worst case of those worst imaginings can be found in antiporn crusader Catharine MacKinnon's *Feminism Unmodified*.[21] In the book's concluding effort to get across what she believes women's everyday lives are like in the world MacKinnon imagines, a world where pornography is widely consumed and where all sexuality is pornography, MacKinnon compares women's purportedly constant fear of rape (the stark terror of knowing what *will*, sooner or later, happen to them) to the horrifying experience of the *Challenger* astronauts in the final seconds of their lives. This bizarre comparison is inaccurate and offensive on a number of counts. But it goes to show how the imagined, known-yet-unknown horror of the astronauts' final minutes can be fantas-matically captured for public discourse.

For the most part we have tacitly agreed to believe that the astronauts died instantly in the fireball that engulfed the shuttle. But if one is trying to drive home a point, as MacKinnon is, knowledge of the astronauts' drawn-out deaths (knowledge that we possess but disavow) is still available for rhetorical special effects. What further evidence do we have of this collective dis-avowal? Try asking the people around you how the *Challenger* astronauts died. Almost invariably they will say that they died in the explosion shortly after the launch. This is what I believed too—that is, until I started reading newspaper and magazine accounts of the disaster that were published in the years after the event. Many of these accounts acknowledge that the astronauts may very likely have been alive until the still-pressurized crew cabin hit the water at 200 miles an hour. This information was based on a *Miami Herald* Sunday magazine story that quoted anonymous NASA investigators, as well as books that critically reviewed the Rogers Commission report on the accident, and was thus widely available. It just didn't "take" in the more conscious levels of the social imaginary of the accident; the public began to insist more and more on the astronauts' quick, almost instant, death. As time went on, descriptions like this one from a 1987 *Washington Post* article became increasingly typical: "Seventy-four seconds after liftoff, [McAuliffe] was dead." Or this one from a 1993 Associated Press release on the seventh anniversary of the accident: "*Challenger blew up 73 seconds after lift-off* on Jan. 28, 1986, *killing all* seven crew members, including schoolteacher

Sharon Christa McAuliffe" (emphasis mine).

The transcript of a "secret NASA tape" of the astronauts plunging to their deaths circulated on the Internet recently and represents yet another collective attempt to both invoke and disavow the horror of those last moments. Bearing all the earmarks of urban legend, the anonymous introduction to the text at first presents it as an actual tape transcript of the astronauts' voices as "they screamed, cried, cursed and prayed for three hellish minutes before they slammed into the Atlantic and perished." But further along we are told that the "transcript" has been assembled from NASA employees' recollections of what they heard at the time and have since discussed among themselves over the years. So we already have the distancing from the source common to urban legend ("My cousin knows someone"—never "I know someone"—"who washed her poodle and put it in the microwave to dry") and a story, like many urban folktales, about a human encounter with technology that ends disastrously.[22] The tape is said not to be the official NASA tape but the one that came from (of course) Christa McAuliffe's personal flight recorder, which the introduction claims was recovered after the disaster—another internal contradiction as to the source of the text. And, as a further sure sign of the folkloric mythmaking nature of the text, it depicts the astronauts, knowing that they are going to die when they hit the water, finding time to hold each other's hands and recite the Lord's Prayer.[23]

Our collective resistance to knowing or believing what happened to McAuliffe and the other *Challenger* astronauts is bound up with the kind of fantasy work anthropologist Michael Taussig calls the "public secret." In recent work on "the political use of controlled delirium or the role of imagination in history," Taussig introduced the idea of a secret that is generally known by everybody but cannot be spoken.[24] A public secret—like the fact that the spirits in a Tierra del Fuego village that Taussig studied are just the men in the village covered in paint and masks—may serve, he says, as crucial social glue: the men act as gods, the women act their belief, and the men act their belief in the women's belief, thus creating the spiritual world that supports the whole of their culture. But some people always pay more than others for keeping the secret. In Taussig's example, the men in the village keep the secret because it is their prerogative and privilege to do so—who doesn't want to be treated like a god? The women, however, keep the secret because they have been threatened with death if they do not.

Like Taussig's public secret, the information about what happened to the *Challenger* astronauts and the sheer pointlessness of McAuliffe's death—two imbricated public secrets—is open and public. But we have collectively, fantasmatically developed a way not to register it. The media, teachers, school counselors, child therapists, parents—all of us—want bodies to be inviolate and death to have meaning, so it is not just a matter of a NASA coverup. Rather, we have entered into an implicit agreement not to let ourselves know. But perhaps the public secret of the event and the crew deaths is no longer serving (if it ever did) to ensure a necessary social cohesiveness, or perhaps the secret(s) need to be collectively divulged because here, as in Tierra del Fuego, it is women who are paying the dearest price.

"ALL UP AND DOWN THE FLORIDA COAST"

Almost every month the Kennedy Space Center gets calls from people who believe they have found a piece of *Challenger*. Even though 90 percent of the spaceship, and the remains of the astronauts and their personal effects, were all recovered in the most comprehensive underwater search ever carried out, and even though what is left (half the external fuel tank and a fourth of the satellite payload) is now under 1,000 feet of water and far too heavy to wash ashore, people still keep trying to put the parts back together. Calvin Burch, the space center's chief of security, who is in charge of checking out all the alleged *Challenger* debris, expressed sympathetic understanding of this ritual phenomenon when he said, "It's still, I think, in the minds of people that that event occurred."[25]

This ritual effort to find and reconstitute the body of the woman and the spaceship echoes the search for Amelia Earhart and her plane, a quest that has been enthusiastically pursued for over fifty years now. In one story an Irish magistrate found Earhart's bones on a Pacific island and set sail to Fiji with the bones in a gunnysack to get positive identification. When the magistrate died during the trip, superstitious sailors threw the gunnysack overboard. In another outcome, Earhart and her navigator were captured by the Japanese before the outbreak of World War II, and escaped, but no one knows to where. In yet another version, she was captured and executed as a spy by the Japanese. The hunt for Earhart took a new turn in 1992 when a team of aviation buffs using sophisticated sonar technology—first employed in the search for parts of the *Challenger*— supposedly found a piece of Earhart's plane and one of her size-nine shoes on a remote South Pacific island.[26]

But Christa McAuliffe was no Amelia Earhart, no matter how much NASA and the media liked to romanticize her in that way. Actually, a closer aviatrix counterpart is Mildred Doran, a twenty-two-year-old elementary school teacher from Caro, Michigan, who in 1927 flew as a passenger in the ill-conceived and ill-fated Dole "Pineapple Derby." A couple of newspaper editors had talked pineapple king James D. Dole into putting up a $35,000 prize for an air race from Oakland to Oahu to promote aviation, Hawaii, and their newspapers. As with McAuliffe, the schoolteacher got the lion's share of worldwide press coverage and, when she died on one of the six planes that either crashed or developed mechanical problems, she was simultaneously lauded as "the splendid little woman" and lamented as "a sacrifice to adventure." Doran was memorialized in *The Outlook* of August 31, 1927, in words that could still ring true on January 28, 1986:

> Beyond question courage even to audacity, zeal to accomplish that which man has never done, passion for adventure and discovery—all are part of the American spirit....Yet it must not be allowed to peril uselessly human life or to degenerate into reckless dashes for prizes and newspaper sensationalism. We learn by disaster; we must not discourage the taking of risks when great things are to be done; but we must enforce precaution against the wagering of life wildly or ignorantly.[27]

We can best remember Christa McAuliffe by also remembering Mildred Doran.

But is it completely right to say that Christa McAuliffe was no Amelia Earhart? Recent revisionist biographies of Earhart show that her aeronautics career was as opportunistically stage-managed and publicity-driven as McAuliffe's. Earhart herself was careful never to overstate her skills, preferring to present herself as a competent and experienced pilot rather than an extraordinary one. But the hype orchestrated by her publishing magnate husband, G.P. Putnam, who had published Charles Lindbergh's story of his famous transatlantic flight, contributed to what now seems a typical backlash against technologically adventurous women. Rumors about Earhart's limited qualifications to fly swirled around her for her entire career. Although she had accumulated a record amount of flying time and had remarkably few accidents, every technological failure she experienced was deemed to be further evidence of her allegedly fraudulent skills. Putnam's packaging of Earhart began when a wealthy socialite sought him out to find a woman to fly the Atlantic solo on a good will mission from America to England. But Earhart felt that during his initial interview with her, Putnam was looking for more than a woman with a pilot's license. He grilled her about her education, work, and hobbies rather than her flying ability, even asking her to talk to make sure she did not drop her "g's" or use "ain't."[28]

Earhart and McAuliffe both chafed at their handlers' manipulations. Both tried to renegotiate their manufactured celebrity image to make it better serve their own personal and political wishes. The most salient similarity between Earhart and

McAuliffe, however, may lie in the kind of feminism they represented, or were asked to represent, even though they were generations apart. In *Still Missing: Amelia Earhart and the Search for Modern Feminism*, Susan Ware argues that Earhart's brand of liberal feminism was the only kind of feminism available to American women in the postsuffrage 1930s. Liberal feminism takes for granted a society in which the sexes are equal and promotes the achievements of extraordinary individual women who can serve as role models for other women, to prove to them that women can do anything that men can. Amelia Earhart used her celebrity to spread this message in lectures throughout America. Christa McAuliffe, as a social studies teacher, taught this idea in a class she developed on the role and history of women in the United States, "The American Woman." With no political analysis of women's subordination and no distinct ideology, liberal feminism is the least threatening and most palatable because so innocuous and the one most suited to promoting the idea that sexual inequality is a thing of the past.

The "already equal" premise of liberal feminism is somewhat more plausible when set in the twenty-third century. A delightful 1995 episode of *Star Trek: Voyager*, the third television spinoff of the original series and the first with a female captain, has Captain Janeway discovering a cryogenically frozen Amelia Earhart, long ago transported to a planet many lightyears from Earth. Once defrosted, Earhart becomes great friends with the Captain, and they share stories of their mutual passion for flying. Reluctantly, they part company at the end of the episode.

REMEMBERING

If, as the NASA chief of security says, "It's still...in the minds of people that that event occurred," how did that event get so deeply into the minds of people in the first place? And how is it being remembered or imagined? As a collective public trauma for children, the *Challenger* disaster ranks very high. Measuring and assessing children's responses to seeing and hearing about the explosion is still an academic growth industry.[29] Not only were classrooms all over the country wired into the broadcast, thousands of teachers were deeply invested in the Teacher in Space program. Over 11,000 teachers had applied to fly on *Challenger* and many others had prepared their students to follow the mission and McAuliffe's lessons from space with NASA-disseminated classroom materials.

Lenore Terr, a researcher on childhood trauma, claims that "virtually every child on both coasts of America was affected by [the *Challenger* disaster]."[30] In her terms, it was an "external event," that is viewed or heard about from a distance, not experienced in one's own life, like the death of a parent or close relative. But what made it more like an internal event was the closeness many children felt to Christa McAuliffe, a stand-in for their own teachers. In this case NASA's attempt to make the space program popular with young people all across America literally blew up in its face. Terr shows that the effect of the disaster was so strong because it hooked into already existing fears spurred by a death in the family, scary movies, ubiquitous missing children ads, or the killings and kidnappings reported on the nightly news. The children she studied brought the explosion into their own homes, developing new fears of exploding house-heaters or ominous hot-water tanks. They also tried to cope with the trauma through fantasy:

> More than half of the kids on both coasts imagined, pretended, and daydreamed their way through the aftermath. Many identified with how it felt to die—to blow up, to be torn apart. They "blew up" as they sat in their classrooms or lay in their beds. Many imagined happier endings—Christa and her colleagues landing on a desert island [shades of Amelia Earhart's Pacific atoll!], or even finding some safe haven in space. A few kids tried to redesign the shuttle—to mentally engineer their way out of the disaster. (328)

Terr bases her claim that virtually every child in America was affected by the *Challenger* disaster on the fact that "almost every single kid could tell me exactly where he or she had been standing or sitting at the time he or she saw or heard about the explosion. The kids almost uniformly claimed they could draw chalk marks on the spots" (329). The vast majority of children could also remember two or three people who had been near them when they saw or heard about the disaster. About two or three in ten could even remember exactly what he or she had been wearing. It is no wonder, she says that "so many of us can remember just where we were standing or sitting when we heard that John F. Kennedy was shot." Terr concludes by saying, "It is apparently the nature of shock-related memory to be set into a certain space" (329). She speculates that, from an evolutionary perspective, our vivid positional sense in connection with shock is a holdover from a primitive need to be instantaneously aware of where one stood when suddenly confronted by a wooly mammoth or a saber-toothed tiger—that's the only way to picture the quickest escape route.[31]

Ulric Neisser, a psychologist who investigates memory in natural contexts, including people's memories of public disasters like the Kennedy assassination and the *Challenger* explosion, has an entirely different understanding of this "positional sense."[32] The day after the explosion, Neisser and his graduate student Nicole Harsch asked 104 college students to give a detailed account of how they had heard about the event. Forty-four of the same students again gave their recollections thirty-two months later. Six months after that, forty members of this group again recalled the event, and were asked to rate the vividness of their memories. The researchers found that even though most of the students described their memories as vivid, more than a third of their recollections of specific aspects of the event were wildly different from their original accounts. Even when the interviewers tried to jog the student's memory by showing them a copy of their original report, none of those with discrepant recollections were able to retrieve their original memories. This study tells us a great deal about the mechanics of memory retrieval, but it also suggests a greater reach of fantasy than Terr allows. Fantasy is not just a mental tool employed to work through trauma; the memory of the trauma is itself a fantasy, a story the subject tells retrospectively to resist or rework the knowledge of an experience. All stages of remembering a collective trauma like the *Challenger* disaster are shot through with fantasy.

In a somewhat more anecdotal study, I asked students in my spring 1992 science-fiction-film course at the University of California at Santa Barbara to write something for me about their memories of the *Challenger* disaster. About thirty of seventy students (mostly male, as is typical with this course) responded. Not surprisingly, they ranked the *Challenger* explosion as the most traumatic public event of their lives (most of my students were in ninth and tenth grade when it happened), as traumatic, they thought, as the John F. Kennedy assassination had been for their parents. But they also told me some unexpected things. Some of the respondents said, for instance, that they resented all the attention that had been given to Christa McAuliffe since she wasn't even a professional astronaut. But what really surprised me was the number of them that reported being in science class at the time. They went on to tell how this ironic coincidence had profoundly changed their relation to science; several professed to having lost faith in the discipline at that moment. It seems improbable, however, that so many of them were actually in science class at the time. Perhaps the students wanted or needed that irony to rationalize a changed relation to science and technology, as well as to their own futures.

Much more could be added to support the claim that the *Challenger* explosion was a collective trauma that continues to affect many Americans. Such evidence, however, would need to be qualified by clarifying exactly who is meant by "us." Not every classroom in America, for example, could afford the televisions used to view the disaster. Nor was everyone successfully interpellated as a horrified, concerned citizen. Still, the Reagan administration tried its best to turn the accident into patriotic fodder (much to the disgust of the astronauts' families and many others), and the networks seized on the catastrophe as another opportunity to show how the media can unify us (or create an "us") in our collective national grief.

Efforts to commemorate the tragedy of the *Challenger* astronauts' deaths have since turned into a comedy of errors. In 1989 New Hampshire citizens found themselves squabbling over a proposal to build a million-dollar monument to McAuliffe at a time when the state was cutting dental care and other services for children. The state finally settled on constructing a much more fitting "living memorial," a planetarium rather than a statue. In Florida, a campaign to raise money through license tag sales for an astronauts memorial at the Kennedy Space Center was investigated for "errant spending policies." Worst of all, when the memorial was finally constructed in 1991, the massive wall of black granite, which tilts its face to the Florida skies (it is called the Space Mirror), immediately developed cracks where the names of the fallen astronauts are carved. A few weeks later the entire monument was declared a safety hazard and closed to visitors.

But surely the macabre *Challenger* astronaut tomb at Arlington National Cemetery represents the most ill-conceived attempt to remember McAuliffe and her fellow astronauts. Arlington began as a place to bury unknown soldiers or those whose families could not afford the cost of private burial services. But now it is the great American cemetery, the symbolic last resting place for America's military heroes. Unintentionally disquieting, the *Challenger* monument marks the spot where the remaining parts of the astronauts' bodies were buried after the identifiable remains were turned over to the families for private services. This attempt to sacralize the astronauts and to treat their body parts as saintly relics, seems rather to evoke feelings of awkwardness and embarrassment, as if no one wants to think about those dismembered bodies back together again, encapsulated in a common grave. A former Arlington tour guide offered a salient example of public disavowal when he told me that the cemetery administration doesn't tell the guides what to say about the *Challenger* monument. The guides, in their own awkwardness, then, tend not to say anything about what, precisely, is buried there. Cracking nervous jokes, they quickly try to move the tour groups to other sites.

REPEATING

Remembering, as Freud said in "Remembering, Repeating and Working-Through," is not so much about filling in gaps but overcoming the resistances due to repression.[33] The most important job of the analyst, the "art of interpretation," is to recognize those resistances when and where they appear. But sometimes it is possible to remember something only through acting it out: "He reproduces it not as a memory but as an action; he *repeats* it, without, of course, knowing that he is repeating it" (150). This unconscious compulsion to repeat is everywhere apparent in our individual and collective attempt to deal with the *Challenger* disaster and with the death of the woman-teacher-astronaut. What else could explain ABC correspondent Morton Dean's choice of words when covering the first shuttle launch to follow the disaster, two years later. As the rising spacecraft approached the point where the *Challenger* had exploded, he intoned, "The shuttle is passing through its most challenging moment." Or the decision of the organizers planning the opening ceremonies for the new Challenger Memorial Education Center at Cape Kennedy, who thought a more hi-tech ribbon-cutting would be a good idea: instead of using scissors, they put a small explosive charge on the ribbon. Onlookers and the press watched in horror and astonishment as the columns of smoke rose and the tattered ribbons trailed to the ground, exactly, if inadvertently, reproducing the image of the *Challenger* exploding in the sky. Or the Building Blaster series of toys that indulged children in their compulsion to repeat by offering them a variety of structures to build and then blow up—warehouses, highrises, and, most notoriously, a space shuttle. Parents who found this toy concept both disturbing and tasteless lobbied Sears and Toys 'Я' Us to remove the Building Blaster space shuttle from the shelves. But it is possible that children were not simply "acting out" (engaging in unconscious repetition) destructively by repeatedly blowing up the space shuttle. Like the children Lenore Terr studied who tried to mentally reengineer the space shuttle so that it would never fail, it is likely that the Building Blaster kids were not so much building the shuttle so they could blow it up as blowing it up so they could rebuild it. Parents who nixed their children's play with the toy were probably acting more on their own unconscious fears and tastes than in response to the symbolic work their children might have been doing with this plastic representation of the shuttle.

Even NASA has been unable to avoid repeating the disaster for the sake of entertainment. One of the most popular exhibits at the new Space Center Houston, a $70 million attraction designed by the same firm that did Disney's Epcot Center, is a Nintendo-like exhibit that is a wall of computer simulators the visitor can use to attempt to land the space shuttle. The exhibit area resonates with loud crashing sounds when, as is the case more often than not, the visitor veers into the swamp or explodes on the runway.

Why would NASA want to deliberately activate this horrific repetition as an attraction in its space theme park? Science fiction writer James Gunn claims that the *Challenger* disaster was the best thing that had happened to NASA in a long time. In a 1974 essay, Gunn had already predicted that the greatest threat to NASA's popularity would be its increasing mundanity—no more poetry, no more *human* adventure.[34] He says the *Challenger* disaster and the deaths of the seven astronauts have made NASA a more popularly appealing science fiction story, giving back to the agency an aura of risk, heroism, and excitement about the unknown.

Michel Serres argues that the *Challenger* disaster is itself a repetition of a very particular kind and that the felt horror is a screen affect. In *Statues*, he places the *Challenger* explosion in a long tradition of public sacrifices and funeral pyres.[35] Serres calls the shuttle "a Trojan horse taking off for the moon, a red bull charging into space. An idol or rocket as tomb."[36] We need these ritual sacrifices, he says, to retain and pretend to go beyond our links with antiquity. The ancients deliberately sacrificed humans;

we make ourselves believe it was just an accident. We do it, he says, because science and technology have now become the motor of history, and the politics of science has now taken the place of politics itself. The staging of a primitive ritual sacrifice like the *Challenger* "accident" is one way to try to bring science back to myth, to religion, to be able to confront our rational technological knowledge with our ethical and religious uneasiness about it. Or, as *Forbidden Planet's* Captain Adams (Leslie Nielsen) says after Dr. Morbius and the Krell mind-over-matter machines have been spectacularly destroyed for their technological hubris, "[That's why] we have laws and religion."

French theorist Paul Virilio also argues that a catastrophic accident like the *Challenger* disaster is never "just" an accident.[37] Every technology carries its risks: as soon as we have ships we have shipwrecks, with trains we have derailments, cars bring carwrecks and electricity electrocution. To overlook the fallibility of technology is "to practice dissimulation, ensure disinformation, and so contribute to a loss of confidence in the effects of science" (81). He urges exposing the accident in order not to be exposed to it, making room in public information for *fallibility*. Virilio's proposed solution is to establish a museum of accidents, one dedicated to showing objects that are exploding or decomposing rather than objects that stimulate a morbid curiosity on the part of the visitor that could turn into a new romanticism of technological ruin. In the end, he concludes that this "museum of accidents" already exists: the TV. In contrast to the television-as-wasteland school of criticism, Virilio is suggesting that television is not just a vehicle for the compulsion to repeat but a machine that can be used to work through our rich and strange desire for scenarios of technological failure, what Susan Sontag called "the imagination of disaster."[38]

If the *Challenger* disaster has been compulsively repeated, so has the mismanagement of the meanings of women in space. To understand that the treatment of McAuliffe was no anomaly or exception, it is illustrative to consider the case of Roberta Bondar, the first Canadian woman in space, whose *Discovery* mission was launched on January 22, 1992. Bondar just wanted to be seen as a qualified and competent doctor-scientist-astronaut, but everyone wanted her to represent something for them. NASA, in yet another effort to imbue itself with *Star Trek*–like multiculturalism, released a picture of Bondar dressed up in a Royal Canadian Mounties uniform posing with fellow *Discovery* astronaut Norman Thagard, a graduate of Florida State University, decked out as the university's (controversial) mascot, Seminole Chief Osceola. Bondar said she didn't mind, especially "given the choice of dressing up perhaps as a beaver or as a Mountie."[39] And though the Canadian Space Agency strongly objected to the photograph's dissemination to the media (probably because of its cheesy chauvinism), NASA distributed it anyway. The decision to pair a stereotypically Canadianized Bondar with an astronaut costumed as an American "Indian" was perhaps inspired by President Bush's desire to present an image of U.S.-Canadian unity in the aftermath of the controversial Free Trade agreement. The president phoned Bondar as *Discovery* was passing over Canada and told her to "keep up the good work" and say hello to his "friend Brian Mulroney."

As the first Canadian woman to circle the globe, Bondar was expected to represent not only Canada's participation in the global community but also the unity of Canada, at a moment when Québec secessionist fervor was at its peak. Bondar dutifully reported that when she looked down on Canada from the shuttle (and took corroborative pictures with the Canadian-developed IMAX camera), "It was borderless, a continuum from sea to sea. There were no lines on the map....I saw it as a united part, and I felt proud." In a Canadian radio broadcast she compared the constitutional debates going on in Canada to a *Star Trek* episode and suggested that her nation needed the kind of unity and tolerance preached by that television show.[40]

Bondar's ravaged, deindustrialized hometown of Sault Ste. Marie enjoyed a brief period of "Bondar-mania." One citizen proclaimed, "Roberta Bondar is helping us get over some bad times and make us feel better about being here." The town's Algoma Steel Corporation had just "restructured" itself, laying off hundreds of workers. But during Bondar-mania, concession stand business was brisk, selling Bondar Burgers, Discovery Dogs, and Shuttle Sausages. Another citizen said, "Roberta has shown us that anyone can achieve anything they desire, even a woman."[41] Canadian women scientists and engineers also wanted Bondar to represent them, especially in the wake of the traumatic massacre of fourteen women engineering students at the University of Montreal in 1989. Some women scientists objected to the lesbian and gay appropriation of Bondar (queer lore about Bondar was rampant), pointing out that having no children, not wearing makeup, and favoring rugby shirts for almost every occasion did not make her a lesbian. Women scientists, they said, are all that way, just too busy for kids, lipstick, and fancy clothes.

Bondar's *Discovery* mission was considered one of the most successful in terms of the results of the experiments carried out on board, but the flight itself was surrounded by controversial publicity, most of it involving Bondar's role as a *woman* in space. Canadians responded angrily to a *Toronto Star* headline that said Bondar was doing "housework" on the *Discovery* shuttle, giving the impression that the accomplished scientist was serving as maid for the male astronauts. Tidying up, the Canadian Space Agency quickly retorted, is an important activity for all astronauts. The most controversial moment, however, came when the *Discovery* astronauts chose to substitute Bondar for the coin in the coin toss for the Super Bowl game that was taking place during their mission. "Flipped" by two male astronauts, she spun while curled in a fetal position, literally a token woman in space. Although some Canadians found this tasteless and sexist, Bondar's hometown newspaper said it showed what a "good sport" she was.[42]

Bondar accomplished her job fearlessly and professionally but still expressed regret at the public reception: "It doesn't matter what my qualifications are, all people will see are my pierced ears."[43] Bondar quit the Canadian Space Agency in 1992, saying she wanted to get more involved in medical research. (A Canadian Press release in 1996 reported that no Canadian university had yet given her a permanent research base—four years after her flight.) But the Canadian women's magazine *Chatelaine*, which voted Bondar 1993 "Woman of the Year," reported that pique may also have played a part in her decision to leave. Bondar was reportedly still furious that NASA allowed her fellow astronauts' wives and children to greet them after their shuttle flight while she had to "plead" to have her mother admitted.[44] Bondar had always claimed that what she liked about NASA was that women were not given "special treatment."[45] But in more ways than one, this woman astronaut *was* given special treatment.

The example of Roberta Bondar would suggest that as late as 1992 NASA had learned very little about how to manage the meanings of women in the space program. One lesson that NASA did "learn," was one that was ultimately not very helpful for women in space. In looking at the abilities and credentials of some recent women in the astronaut corps one might think that NASA quietly responded to McAuliffe's lack of qualifications by cynically recruiting only "token overachievers" (a familiar tactic often used for hiring women at other U.S. industries and corporations). Take Mae Jemison, for example, the doctor-astronaut who flew on the 1992 *Endeavor* voyage and the first African-American woman in space. Her list of accomplishments is astonishing: she studied chemical engineering and African and Afro-American studies at Stanford, then went on to medical school at Cornell. After receiving her medical degree in 1981, she became a Peace Corps medical officer for Sierra Leone and Liberia. She was working as a general practitioner and attending graduate engineering courses in Los Angeles when NASA tapped her in 1987. She is fluent in six languages and is an artist. At the time she was recruited, she was the only African-American woman among NASA's 92 astronauts. It looks as if NASA is limiting the involvement of women—especially minority women—in the astronaut corps by making them demonstrate markedly more qualifications than male candidates. Another example: Julie Payette, who is preparing to become Canada's second woman astronaut, is a research engineer in computer sciences, a linguist who is fully bilingual in French and English, a musician who can sing and play piano and flute, a triathlete, *and* a trapeze artist. What more do women have to do to show that they are capable of flying through the air?

We have seen how sick jokes responded to the collective public trauma of the *Challenger* disaster by transforming it into humorous vignettes that are ultimately stories of female trouble. But these jokes also bear a remarkable resemblance to apocryphal tales that earlier kept women out of the pilot's seat and the space program. The head of NASA's medical services in Houston tells one story to show how things are better for women than they used to be in past decades: a woman pilot, who was found to be menstruating, was blamed when a plane she was flying lost a wing. But he admits that to this day NASA medical officers are frequently asked how it is that menstruating women can go into space, as if men too did not have fluids in their bodies that regularly need to be released.[46]

In 1973 *Ms.* magazine published a cover story by Joan McCullough on NASA's efforts to keep women out of the space program. In the late 1950s twenty-five women pilots, several of whom had logged at least 8,000 hours of flying time (this was all commercial flying time since women were not allowed to fly jets), were asked to participate in the medical and psychological tests for the Mercury training program. After thirteen of them had passed the same examinations John Glenn and Alan Shepard had taken (who had, respectively, 5,000 and 2,900 hours of flying time), the program for women was abruptly curtailed. The women pilots had been found to be more resistant to radiation, less subject to heart attacks, and better able to endure extremes of heat, cold, pain, noise, and loneliness. Since they weighed less than the men and required less food and oxygen, they would also have saved money in the expensive per-pound business of capsule launching. But none of that mattered: NASA decreed, No Women. In 1963, after the Soviets' launching of a female astronaut, a NASA spokesman referred to it as "just a publicity stunt." Another NASA spokesman said bluntly, "Talk of an American spacewoman makes me sick."

McCullough's *Ms*. magazine piece also documented NASA's discrimination against the women who applied for the scientific slots in the program. In 1967, seventeen women with advanced degrees in fields directly related to space were among those reviewed by the 900-member, all-male science selection panel. The women were all bypassed for eleven men, including four men in their twenties and four others who had not yet obtained doctorates.

Now you might be saying to yourself, that was the bad old days, surely things are better now. But there are many ways in which NASA is still repeating itself, unable to think about women in space. For example, for mixed crews of men and women to spend lengthy amounts of time in space, on a space station or on the Mission to Mars , extensive behavioral, psychological, and physiological studies need to be done. But NASA has steadfastly refused to conduct these studies because they might involve touchy issues of sex and sexuality. One anthropologist was fired from a NASA consulting team for merely raising the importance of carrying out such studies if women are going to be part of long-range space exploration. And a 1992 *New York Times* article on sex in space cited the audacity of Dr. Yvonne Clearwater, head of habitability research at NASA's Ames Research Center, who said agency scientists and officials at work on the space station's design had an obligation "not to serve as judges of morality but to support people in living as comfortably and normally as possible."[47] A colleague, speaking on condition of anonymity, said this statement just about killed Clearwater's career.

In the same article the editor of *Ad Astra*, the magazine of the National Space Society, says that the topic of sexuality in space is increasingly important but "hard to discuss intelligently, given the agency's reluctance....NASA is so puritanical that the subject is difficult for them to broach." If NASA refuses to study contraceptive techniques in weightlessness, for example, this will ensure that women do not go into space, given the danger and inconvenience of pregnancy in an environment with so many unknown factors.

People are still trying to find reasons why women are physiologically unsuited to going into space. In the fall of 1992, PBS aired a new series on space exploration. One episode, "Quest for Planet Mars," intersperses scenes of NASA tests of men and women for a lengthy Mars voyage with scenes of a simulated trip to Mars. Toward the end of the program, after we have been told of the two to three hours of daily exercise and the regular hormone injections that all astronauts will probably have to endure to prevent decrease in bone mass due to weightlessness, our narrator, Patrick Stewart (who plays Captain Jean-Luc Picard on *Star Trek: The Next Generation*), intones, "Tests on women are only now being done. We won't know until longer tests, perhaps on a space station, whether women lose more bone mass." The implication is that women's different physiology may once again be invoked to keep them from going into space.

"But what about Sally Ride!" is the instant comeback to anyone who questions the way NASA has allowed women to figure in the world of space. Ride, the first American woman in space, was the very model of the cool, professional, and scientifically accomplished astronaut. She gained experience on two shuttle voyages, showed her technical knowledge and tenacious skepticism on the presidential commission that investigated the *Challenger* disaster, and went on to write *Leadership and America's Future in Space*, an important report that outlined NASA's long-range strategies and plans. An article in the *Washington Post* announcing Ride's surprise departure from the space program in 1987 said, however, that although she had been selected after intense competition, she was chosen (I think, like McAuliffe) because she was considered unlikely to display the kind of independence that would cause NASA political problems. But Ride did cause NASA political problems with her sudden resignation. Baffled and dismayed, NASA officials said, "We just can't figure it out. She was a real symbol for us. She did us real proud during the hearings and we assumed she would be one of the first back in space."[48] As usual, Ride shunned publicity, and said very little about her reasons for quitting. But it was not hard to surmise that she had simply lost confidence in NASA.

Mae Jemison's equally sudden departure in 1993 also surprised and even angered some NASA officials. She, too, had been such an important symbol for them, a major player in NASA's effort to look inclusive, to be *popular*. Jemison had lectured widely on the space program and was generous in giving interviews, for which she was much in demand.

NASA lost Ride, Jemison, and Bondar in rapid succession following the more profound losses of Resnick and McAuliffe. In "Now Voyager," a wrenching essay on McAuliffe's death, Ellen Willis speaks of her own anger about women "*losing space*."[49] Although she grew up curious about the stars and space exploration, Willis had lost that interest until NASA enlisted McAuliffe—a woman who, like herself, was a civilian, teacher, and mother. Willis says she was so alienated from the WASP space cowboy version of spaceflight that she missed watching the moon landing on TV: "Did I purposely decide not to watch it? did I forget? did I have a deadline?" No, she decides, like many women she passed it up out of anger that NASA's iconography left her no room for fantasies of women in space.

WORKING-THROUGH

Because of the way in which the particularities of McAuliffe's life and death lend themselves to individual and collective fantasy, her story has become densely inscribed in science fictional, mythical, folkloric, and ideological narratives about women, technology, and catastrophe. How might some of these narratives be rewritten? How can we transform the popular image of woman as the embodiment of technological disaster, as someone who has no place in space? Simply remembering McAuliffe is not enough because remembering, as we have seen, is never simple: we misremember and disremember, select and repress, trivialize and romanticize. We try to commemorate the dead astronauts and instead repeat the trauma. To rewrite the story of women in space, we need to work through the trauma, which involves not just recognizing the resistances to knowing but, in Freud's words, becoming "conversant" with those resistances.

A necessary first step in becoming "conversant" is a decidedly empirical one: NASA must release all the tapes, photographs, and autopsy reports. If, as theorist Eric Santner says, "the work of mourning is an emphatically empirical procedure; mourning without historical knowledge is effectively and affectively empty," then NASA has only compounded its original blunder in not releasing these materials."[50] I have already noted the way our knowing and not knowing how McAuliffe and the other *Challenger* astronauts died has created a psychical void that can be filled with our own worst imaginings, a fraught space of disavowal that can be captured for all sorts of public discourse, from jokes to movies to legal arguments, almost all of them inimical to women. The astronauts' bodies have become an *unspeakable* horror; it is now time to speak about that horror. This desire to know, no matter how shot through with fantasmatic thinking—disavowal, guilt, projection, overidentification, and all the rest—is a desire whose reality and efficacy must be acknowledged. The families of MIAs, of accident and murder victims, even the relatives of those killed by Jeffrey Dahmer want to know, demand to know, in exact and excruciating detail, how their loved ones died. Over and over, they say that they cannot go on, cannot resume their own lives until *they know*. Tell us anyway, they say, no matter how horrible; knowing is infinitely better than not knowing.

Knowing, then, allows mourning to proceed. But it also marks the beginning of being able to rewrite narratives that have become murky, invidious, or otherwise harmful. Other catastrophic events since the *Challenger* disaster offer persuasive evidence of the renarrativizing value of empirical knowledge. Take, for example, the explosion that killed forty-seven sailors on board the battleship *U.S.S. Iowa* in April 1989. A Navy panel investigating the explosion concluded that it had been deliberately set off by Gunner's Mate Clayton Hartwig, whom they characterized as a suicidal loner despairing over an unrequited homosexual love affair with another sailor. This conclusion was based on the most tenuous corroborating evidence and held together merely by what the panel members imagined *must* have been the cause—Hartwig's supposed homosexuality. After long and mighty protests from Hartwig's family, and the outraged disbelief of scientists and psychologists over the Navy's $4 million fabrication of "proof," the Navy panel had to fully recant the charge.

The Hartwig case was only overturned when the Navy considered new tests of the on-site explosives and artillery, tests not driven by a will to peg the disaster to homosexual desire. (And if these new tests had not been done, you can be sure that

Hartwig would have become the Willie Horton of the gays-in-the-military debate.) So, too, independent examination of all the *Challenger* disaster material, when NASA finally releases it, will allow another public story to be told, one not about the courageous, martyred astronauts meeting a quick, "clean," even spectacular death. But the point here is not to refute fantasmatic thinking with empirical evidence or to try to solve mysteries by replacing fantasies with facts. This is so even though a good part of the solution to the puzzle of the *U.S.S. Iowa* explosion and the *Challenger* crew deaths was to counter a politically inflected interpretation of events with better science—a better analysis with better evidence. Rather the issue is to demand better science while acknowledging the work of fantasy in everyday life, popular culture, and scientific practice. In the end, one can get at the empirical only through understanding the omnipresence of fantasmatic thought.

Freud gives a good example of the necessity of being able to do two things at once—that is, carrying out the search for what really happened while acknowledging the work of fantasy—when he cites the simultaneously high incidence of child sexual abuse *and* of infantile sexual fantasy. Many contemporary investigators refuse Freud's insight, however, and repeatedly fail to discover and help the children who have actually been abused. Case after case is overturned because of flawed interviewing techniques that tap straight into children's unconscious fears, desires, and ongoing sexual theorizing. If child sexual abuse investigators could accept that children have sexual fantasies, they could use this knowledge to refine their interviewing tech-

niques. Demanding that children always be "innocent," even in
their unconscious lives, means not only that some adults will be
falsely charged but also that investigators will not be able to tell
when children are describing actual abuse. As with efforts to
reconfigure the narratives of McAuliffe and the *Challenger* disaster, the aim here is not to separate fact from fantasy but to show
how each embodies a distinct kind of knowledge and how one is
deeply implicated in the other. Both kinds of knowledge deserve
to be evaluated without one cancelling the other.

Judging from the way the Navy handled the investigation
into the fatal October 1994 crash of Lieutenant Kara Hultgreen's
F-14, even the Navy might have learned a little bit about becoming conversant with its resistances. Almost immediately after
Hultgreen, the first woman qualified as an F-14 combat pilot,
crashed into the ocean while trying to land on an aircraft carrier,
Southern California news organizations began receiving anonymous faxes, supposedly from disgruntled male aviators, raising
questions about her test results and accusing the Navy of giving
preferential treatment to women to erase the stain of the Tailhook
sexual harassment scandal. Right-wing talk radio shows buzzed
for days with callers saying, "See, this is what comes of affirmative action." This in turn helped to lay some pseudo-populist
groundwork for Governor Pete Wilson's attempt to repeal state
and university affirmative action programs a few months later, as
part of his ill-fated presidential campaign. The Navy quickly
responded by allowing Hultgreen's mother, at her request, to
release her daughter's test scores, all ranging from average to
above average, with a ranking of third among the seven pilots of

her "Top Gun" class. As Hultgreen's mother put it, "The way I look at it is, being a slightly above-average F-14 pilot is like being a slightly above-average Phi Beta Kappa."[51] According to the tacit double standard to which women are held, however, Hultgreen should have been eligible to fly only if she had achieved the *highest* score in the class; generally, men are allowed to fall somewhere in the middle and still be thought to be qualified but women are not. The report on the accident by the Navy's legal staff exonerated Hultgreen, blaming instead spot valve problems that all too frequently cause F-14 engines to stall. But then the Navy took an important next step by issuing an internal document, a Mishap Investigation Report, based on findings made *after* the recovery of Hultgreen's body and the plane's wreckage in the Pacific. In contrast to the legal staff, this investigative group of six aviators, including three officers from Hultgreen's squadron, concluded that she had contributed to the fatal crash by failing to line up directly on the center line of the landing deck. They found that her last-minute attempt to correct this misalignment had somehow caused her engine to stall. (All of this happened in only four seconds but it was enough for her radar intercept officer to be ejected safely; Hultgreen was the only fatality.) By fully investigating the accident and making public damning or even conflicting documents, the Navy responded in a way Hultgreen would have demanded. She had always warned her superiors against being lenient toward women, saying, "Guys like you have to make sure there's only one standard."[52]

To the Navy's credit, it kept to only one standard, even though, following Tailhook, it would have been better public relations to stop after the first report found the woman utterly blameless. The second investigating team also took care to put the accident in context, reminding the public just how talented and competent a pilot had been lost: Hultgreen ranked first in defending the fleet from simulated attacks by enemy aircraft and in air refueling, and second in tactics to evade enemy aircraft and in combined familiarization with tactics and aircraft. According to their report, she had a total of 1,242 hours of flying time and fifty-eight carrier landings, including seventeen night landings. Hultgreen got no "special treatment," then, only the scrutiny and respect that would have been given any able pilot. As was her due, this pilot, with an aerospace engineering degree who had wanted to be an astronaut, was buried at Arlington.

There have been many similar attempts since 1986 to "work-through" the trauma of the *Challenger* disaster, attempts that have ranged from the practical to the creative. These have met with varying degrees of success, if one defines "success" as becoming conversant with the resistances so that other stories, other institutional and popular narratives, can be written about women in space. One way of trying to get around the daunting project of rewriting those stories has been to evade the issue altogether, saying that women should not be in space—or men either. These arguments for abandoning space are familiar and quite plausible: we cannot afford it (each shuttle launch costs at least a billion dollars); space exploration is based largely on a military demand for it; the relatively inexpensive "unmanned" spacecraft gather much more hard scientific data than the "manned" vessels; we should not waste money on going to Mars when we do not have decent contraceptive technology or adequate funding for day care on Earth. But this kind of thinking, Ellen Willis says, is just one more version of the bread-before-roses, keep-our-noses-to-the-grindstone mentality that maintained, "we shouldn't go to rock and roll concerts while a war is going on; we shouldn't worry about sexual happiness till we've gotten rid of capitalism," and so on.

If NASA can remain a civilian agency, reemphasize science over engineering, get a grip on the contractors (those O-rings are still dicey), continue to share research with the former Soviets who have vastly more knowledge in areas like long-term space habitation, forge a truly multinational space station project, work more closely with universities along the lines of the successful Caltech supervision of the Jet Propulsion Laboratory, and give as much emphasis to Mission to Planet Earth through developing the Earth Observation System as to the Mission to Mars then "going into space" could again become a bright and laudable effort that would deserve the support and involvement of America's best scientists, engineers, and technicians. But that is a lot of ifs—and some strategic additions to the list are crucial. A knowledge of the history of NASA would suggest, if not dictate, that anthropologists, sociologists, and psychologists should be added to the astronaut corps and that the budget for the terrific NASA librarians and historians should be beefed up. And then, why not put public relations under the supervision of the information staffers since they are consistently more knowledgeable, analytical, and forthcoming than any of the official NASA hypesters have been?

What are the chances? NASA is not monolithic; some of the best criticisms have come from scientists and engineers within NASA, who have themselves made most of the above recommendations. The story of physicist Richard P. Feynman's witty and devastating criticisms of NASA whitewashing in the presidential commission report on the *Challenger* accident is just one well-known example. (His brilliantly theatrical gesture of plunging a piece of rubber into a glass of ice water to demonstrate what happens to O-rings in cold temperatures cannot be celebrated enough.) Some of the investigative journalism of NASA has been superb, especially Joseph J. Trento's *Prescription for Disaster: From the Glory of Apollo to the Betrayal of the Shuttle*.[53] Historians of science and organizational studies scholars are beginning to produce analyses of the scientific and corporate culture of NASA, most notably sociologist Diane Vaughn's *The Challenger Launch Decision: Risky Technology, Culture, and Deviance at NASA* (1996), published on the tenth anniversary of the disaster.[54] But most useful for understanding NASA's public face and its popular role is Eric J. Chaisson's *The Hubble Wars* (1994), a book whose undertitle says it all, *Astrophysics Meets Astropolitics in the Two-Billion-Dollar Struggle over the Hubble Space Telescope*.[55] Chaisson is a senior scientist at the Space Telescope Science Institute, established by NASA at the urging of the National Academy of Sciences to serve as the scientific nerve center of the *Hubble* space mission. As both an astronomer and a director of educational programs, Chaisson is uniquely positioned to provide a critical perspective on the way NASA does big science and big public relations. He was not the first to say that while most government agencies have a public relations office, NASA is a public relations office that has an agency. After witnessing NASA's astonishing unwillingness or inability to communicate its mission or describe what is actually going on at any given time on any given project, Chaisson says he came to understand the Capitol Hill crack that NASA stands for "Never A Straight Answer."

One small misstep by NASA's public relations office shows just how hard it will be for the agency to live down this reputation. In June 1994, the space agency called a press conference to announce, with great fanfare, that a committee had been put together to consider whether to revive the Teacher in Space program. There was, of course, a great deal of media interest in the committee's work. But in the months that followed no report was ever issued on its deliberations or conclusions. Repeated inquiries elicited only this reply: the committee was an internal committee, no one outside of NASA had been consulted, no documents were to be made public, and there were no plans to publicize the committee's work and recommendations. Why would NASA make a public announcement and then not follow up on the interest generated? One can only conclude that whatever other reforms NASA may make, rethinking women in space through taking a hard, public, look at the Teacher in Space program does not seem like one of them. Fortunately, the real reform, the necessary labor of working-through, *is* taking place, not so much within NASA as alongside it, by ordinary people and writers.

In Grace George Corrigan's memoir *A Journal for Christa* (1993),[56] the mother of the teacher-astronaut first offers a dedication to her daughter and an announcement that the book is meant as "a celebration of Christa's life for our children and grandchildren." Later, however, Corrigan tells us that her impulse to write the book came from the journal her daughter started when she was pregnant for the first time. Christa said, "I would have loved it if my mother had said, 'Here, Christa, this is what my life was like.'" The book, then, is a memoir of McAuliffe's life folded into a story of her mother's life. This understanding goes a long way toward explaining the impulse and strategy of *A Journal for Christa*: a relentless attempt on Corrigan's part to get her daughter back—from NASA, from legend—by giving a more personal meaning to Christa's death and life. Christa died heroically, her mother argues, because she had been heroic all her life, as a daughter, mother, wife, teacher, and citizen. It was a heroicism born of middle-class normality.

The heavily illustrated book contains only one small image of McAuliffe in NASA uniform (this official NASA photograph is also reproduced on the book jacket). More numerous are the pictures of McAuliffe with her children, students, and Girl Scout troop; at her confirmation, sixteenth birthday, and wedding. We even see her in a nun's costume, playing the part of Sister Margaretta in her senior class play, *The Sound of Music*. This exhaustive *normalizing* of McAuliffe, this re-placing her into the mundanity of private everyday life is a perfectly understandable way for this mother to try to come to terms with the spectacularly public circumstances of her daughter's death. And it does put before readers a version of Christa's heroism that partly resists the one produced by NASA imagineering, even though it ultimately fails to do so because it was precisely that "ordinariness" that formed the bedrock of the PR construction of McAuliffe. Corrigan's strategy, then, was to try to outdo NASA through an even more excessive insistence on ordinariness. Within that ploy, she sought to redefine "ordinariness" away from "representative mediocrity" (with which, presumably, all Americans are supposed to identify) toward the heroism of women's middle-class everyday life (with which Corrigan surely identifies). *This* story of the Teacher in Space may represent a kind of working-through of the trauma for her mother, but something more is needed for the rest of us.

Corrigan tells us that the family made a pact after Christa's death not to give personal interviews to the media, which included not expressing any opinions about NASA. She reveals, however, that after her husband died she found among his papers several handwritten pieces about what he called "NASA's ineptitude." After listing a dozen names of high-ranking NASA officials who had advised against the launch, Ed Corrigan wrote: "My daughter Christa McAuliffe was not an astronaut—she did not die *for* NASA and the space program—she died *because of* NASA and its egos, marginal decisions, ignorance and irresponsibility. NASA betrayed seven fine people who deserved to live"(6). He also noted the statement of one of the Commissioners: "It was no accident; it was a mistake that was allowed to happen."(6) McAuliffe's father said he had been angry since the day Christa was killed. He had observed NASA's ineptitude firsthand, especially at the launch site, but had agreed (along with the other astronauts' spouses and families) to appear loyal to NASA. He therefore disclosed his real feelings only in his private writings, which Corrigan includes in her book, without comment. That she allowed these harsh words and bitter feelings to see the light, even if posthumously, suggests that she was not entirely comfortable with the happy-face, Pollyanna attitude she adopted at NASA's unspoken behest.

So far, the several books written by former women astronauts have contributed little to the work of working-through since most of them have chosen to relate their experiences in the form of stories for children. In these stories, space is as innocent as childhood is presumed to be. The first lines of Sally Ride's book for children, *To Space and Back* (1986) are: "'What's it like to be in space?' 'Is it scary?' 'Is it cold?' 'Do you have trouble sleeping?' These are questions everyone asks astronauts who have been in space."[57] In the introduction, Ride explains that her book was almost ready to go on January 28, 1986, "when the unthinkable happened. The space shuttle *Challenger* exploded one minute after liftoff." After the accident, she says, she thought a lot about the book and whether or not she wanted to change any part of it. She decided to change nothing, except to dedicate the book to the memory of the *Challenger* astronauts and to add a brief mention of the accident to the introduction. Recognizing that the disaster gives new meaning to the first question children ask about space—"Is it scary?"—Ride points out that "all adventures—especially into new territory—are scary." The danger of spaceflight is thus naturalized as the function of adventure itself—eliding, for the sake of the children, all questions of social or institutional dysfunction.

Roberta Bondar's book for children, *On the Shuttle: Eight Days in Space* (1993), focuses more on space science than space adventure. Stereotypes aside, there is a good reason for Bondar having chosen to produce a children's book: the co-author is her sister Barbara, a teacher and librarian who specializes in interdisciplinary learning and psycholinguistics and is the author of over twenty educational books and several films. *On the Shuttle* is Barbara Bondar's eighth book for children and a unique chance to collaborate with an astronaut-scientist-doctor who just happens to be her sister. The book is straightforward and informative, covering such topics as "What keeps the shuttle from falling back to Earth?" and "Our amazing inner ear" (it cannot resist, of course, making a plug for Canada's IMAX camera). Given Bondar's history with NASA, the book is surprisingly gung-ho, but again, this is a children's book, so political commentary and critique are out. One inadvertently political moment is the last photograph, which pictures Bondar's *Discovery* crew members and their "loved ones," all of whom seem to be heterosexual spouses, except for Bondar's sister Barbara. *On the Shuttle* allows Bondar to reauthorize herself as a scientist, doctor, and astronaut, a multidimensional role not precluded by NASA's compulsory heterosexuality.

Sometimes it is easiest to engage the issue of our desires and anxieties around women in space through the form of children's books. Rose Bursik's fictional *Amelia's Fantastic Flight* (1992), ingeniously mixes *Where the Wild Things Are* and the *Magic School Bus* series (especially *Lost in the Solar System*) to craft a magical working-through of the lives and deaths of Amelia Earhart and Christa McAuliffe. "Amelia" is a brown girl who lives in

Monument Valley. She loves airplanes and loves reading about them, so she builds one and travels around the world ("She breezed through Brazil and got a kick out of Kenya"). Although she "malfunctions in Mexico," she makes a few quick repairs to land just in time for dinner and a bedtime story from a book with a space shuttle on the cover. The final image is of the book, a hammer, and bucket of nails with which Amelia will presumably build her own space shuttle, just as she built the airplane in which she flew over six continents. *Amelia's Fantastic Flight* offers children—especially young girls—an imaginative working-through that suggests that the best bet for surviving "malfunctions" is having built the machine yourself.

Although the film *SpaceCamp* (1986) was not created in response to the *Challenger* explosion, it offers another working-through that involves children saving the day and surviving in space through hands-on learning of science and technology. In a major bit of bad timing, this film about an astronaut-teacher and her students who are accidentally launched into space, was completed just before the *Challenger* disaster. The studio debated whether to release it, held the film for a few months, then eventually released it in a limited way. Most critics and audiences seemed to feel, finally, that the decision to release *Spacecamp* was not in bad taste. After all, it shows NASA at its spunky best and has a happy ending—the teacher is injured but survives and the shuttle is piloted to safety by a girl student who, with the teacher's help, overcomes self-doubts about her ability to handle the technology of spaceflight. Again, as with *Amelia's Fantastic Flight* (as well as *The Magic School Bus: Lost in the Solar System*, in which the teacher gets stranded in an asteroid belt but is found by an obnoxiously smart and aggressive girl who is detested by the other kids for those qualities until she takes over the lesson plan and saves them all from death in space), *SpaceCamp* is directed toward girls, especially girls who want to learn science and technology from the ground up. And in every case, the female teacher-astronaut survives all "malfunctions" to continue teaching and mentoring the girl.

There is only one book for adults in English about a female astronaut's experiences in space and on the ground, Helen Sharman's *Seize the Moment: The Autobiography of Britain's First Astronaut* (1993).[58] Written with novelist Christopher Priest, Sharman's narrative is a model of how a woman scientist might effectively negotiate the meanings of women in space, even in the face of outrageously commercial and chauvinistic pressures. Sharman should not have been able to pull off constructing a reasonable public persona as a female astronaut because she had so much going against her. A research technologist in the chocolate section of the R & D department of Mars Confectionery Ltd.(!), she was also pursuing doctoral work at Birkbeck College in London when she responded, on a whim, to a radio ad, "Astronaut wanted—no experience necessary." "The girl from Mars," as she was immediately dubbed by the popular press, competed with over five thousand other Britons for a cosmonaut slot on Project Juno, a Soviet space mission. After grueling psychological and medical tests, confirmation of her scientific abilities and capacity for learning foreign languages, Sharman was the only woman who made it to the four finalists, which earned her the tabloid sobriquet "Token woman." After undergoing even more arduous tests with the Soviets, she was chosen for the Juno mission and spent eighteen hard months at the astronaut training facility outside Moscow. The rigors of the two-country evaluation process make it clear that Sharman was no token woman; she won the competition because she excelled in all the qualities needed to be an astronaut.

Although all the finalists for the Soviet launch were told from the beginning that the British cosmonaut mission was entirely commercial, to be paid for by industrial sponsorships, they could not have been prepared for the financial confusion and media circus that ensued. Antequera Ltd., the company that was set up to administer the selection of the cosmonaut (a process that was to be highly publicized), told the would-be cosmonauts from the start that the company would "own the butt" of the successful candidate. And indeed, as Sharman acknowledges, she did end up with her butt "effectively owned." The finalists were interviewed about their motives for going into space and attitudes to various moral compromises they might have to make for the sake of sponsorship. They were forced to wear "irredeemably naff" jumpsuits (which looked like "cast-offs from a Z-grade science fiction movie") to a televised press conference that Sharman characterizes as "a Monty Python sketch about four boffins who had accidentally entered Miss World...but it wasn't as much fun as it might have been!" At various points during the months ahead, the finances fell through, Antequera was dissolved, the four finalists were left stranded and incommunicado in Russia, and no one was given a straight answer. In her book, Sharman wonders, "Is this how NASA operated? Not a pleasant feeling"(90).

Just as the Apollo astronauts, at least in Tom Wolfe's account, found their own grittily glamorous way of having the Right Stuff by resisting NASA's Spam-in-a-can version of astronaut agency, Sharman discovered that she could finally take some measure of control over her Antequera handlers, the corporate sponsors, and the media. It was a constant struggle, however, made up of many small victories, like the broadcast from space she was asked to do for Interflora, one of the sponsors of the mission. The idea was that she, the only woman on the Soyuz trip to the *Mir* space station, would romantically order flowers for someone on Earth and be televised doing so. Meanwhile, of course, her real chores included running experiments on growing luciferase protein crystals and exposing ceramic oxide films to the vacuum of space. Not wanting to face a romance splashed across the tabloids or to put some hapless recipient through the hassle, she sent roses to her mum, disappointing both the press and the sponsor. But what could they do?

The jacket blurb pitches *Seize the Moment* as "the gripping account of how an 'ordinary' British girl did something extraordinary." But Sharman manages to give ordinariness an entirely different spin from the representative mediocrity imposed on McAuliffe. She readily admits that her ordinary life intrigues and frustrates people, especially journalists assigned to write about her. But she cannot produce a story of injustice, privation, bullying, parental cruelty, or domestic upheavals. Nor can she offer stories of triumphing over hardship to break athletic records or to win scholarships. She is just ordinary: "In every street in every

British town and village you will find someone like me"(48).

Sharman thoughtfully teases out the implications and consequences of this ordinariness but what she does *not* do is make a
national virtue out of her "stable and secure" background. Her
description of her lower middle-class upbringing is just that, a
description. She does not want to make the profound normality
of the first part of her life be *the* quality that made her an astronaut. Nor does she allow her ordinariness to get in the way of
becoming an astronaut. "What is it that happened to you, people
ask, that made you into an astronaut?" she is asked, as if to
imply, "that a quarter-century of ordinariness is not a fit prepa-
ration for a job as unusual as being an astronaut"(49). Sharman's
response is to redefine what are usually seen as the extraordinary qualities needed by an astronaut as very ordinary ones that
many people can and should possess: "What it actually requires
(in no particular order of importance) is good health, fitness, the
ability to get on with other people and to work in a team. In the
special case of the Anglo-Soviet mission in which I took part, it
also required the ability to learn Russian quickly and to have a
degree in a technical subject"(89). This is how she conceives of
that ordinary quality of being able to work in a team: "By this I
don't mean the English jolly hockey-sticks kind of thing....A
space mission would be dangerous if manned exclusively by 'top
gun' fighter-pilot jocks or rugged individualists of the lone-
yachtsman type. If astronauts don't work together, they put each
other's lives in jeopardy"(50).

If ordinariness, then, is simply a quality that everyone should
possess, Sharman nonetheless allows that she is unique in one

way: "There is something that happened to me...that will not happen to most people: one day I climbed into a rocket and flew into space"(49). "Ordinariness," as she defines it, simply means having prepared oneself to be able to take advantage of an opportunity should one become available, to be ready to "seize the moment" as her book's title puts it. Sharman's refusal to define ordinariness in moral or nationalistic terms is as refreshing as the critical eye she casts on the miserably flawed and flaky attempts by others to construct her woman-in-space persona. Here is how Sharman addressed the inevitable comparisons between her and Christa McAuliffe:

[They were] presumably wondering how I felt about the prospect of being blown up....What on earth could I say, sensibly, about the prospect of being blown up in a spectacular launch explosion? However, lying there in those quiet moments before the launch began, thoughts about similarities between Christa McAuliffe and myself did go through my mind. For one thing we were both civilian women and in our different ways we had trained to be cosmonauts while surrounded by media attention. I knew many people in Britain would be watching this launch on TV, just as the *Challenger* launch had caught the attention of millions of ordinary Americans, and in particular were both the focus of much interest from schoolchildren....I wished I could have met and known her before she died, because we would probably have had a lot in common, but it would be pretentious and untrue to say I felt spiritually close to her. (38-39)

Although Sharman realizes that this is the wrong answer for journalists, for her it is the only sensible and honest one.

Halfway through the wonderful ordeal recounted in *Seize the Moment*, Sharman laments, "My job was plainly suffering, my parents had been wondering why I hadn't been up to see them, Kevin, my boyfriend, had more or less given up hope of ever seeing me again, and what about my Ph.D.?" (89). As this quotation suggests, the book is personal, sensible, funny, and sharply critical when it needs to be—especially about the media and the institutional cultures of the national space agencies. Yet, it is still remarkably positive about going into space.

Sharman (or her publisher) pulled off one final coup by getting noted science fiction writer Arthur C. Clarke to write the foreword (a move unmatched since Charles Lindbergh agreed to introduce Michael Collins's 1974 *Carrying the Fire: An Astronaut's Journeys*). Scientist, novelist, Commander of the British Empire, and Chancellor of the International Space University, Clarke takes the occasion to remind readers of an attempt at a principle he announced fifty years ago: in *Prelude to Space* he wrote, "We will take no frontiers into space." He believes this hope has been fulfilled: "Interplanetary imperialism seems an unlikely prospect" (13). He praises *Seize the Moment* for its portrayal of friendships "which transcended accidents of birth and upbringing. Even during the height of the unlamented Cold War, astronauts and cosmonauts were able to maintain sincere personal friendships, sometimes despite the wishes of their superiors"(13). National pride is all right, he says, as long as it is free from arrogance or hostility toward other groups of humans. These comments, as well as the spirit and substance of Sharman's book, constitute a not-so-indirect jab at NASA, an agency fueled by Cold War politics and pervaded by frontier rhetoric.[59] The strength of both Clarke's foreword and Sharman's story is that each productively blends a utopianism about space exploration and its future with a critical edge toward ideological and institutional issues that shape this peculiarly fraught yet potentially liberatory scientific and technological endeavor.

STILL WORKING-THROUGH

We keep circling around the *Challenger* disaster, in a holding pattern around the death of the Teacher in Space, trying to find new angles to approach the working-through of what seems to be a perpetual anxiety about women and technology. We can find some of these new angles in recent fiction. In 1988, two years after the shuttle disaster, British author J.G. Ballard pulled together eight of his stories about the decline of the space age. Originally published between 1962 and 1985, the stories were now rereleased under the title *Memories of the Space Age*. The collection is a necrology of astronauts; one story is even called, "The Dead Astronaut." Over and over, the end of Earth and the effective end of humanity (or the best parts of it) are represented by characters musing over the bodies of dead, decaying, or desiccated astronauts. In "The Cage of Sand" the ships of astronauts who never made it to launching platforms in fixed orbit over Earth circle the dying planet (wiped out by imported Martian viruses), "left in this natural graveyard, forming their own monument."

"The Man Who Walked on the Moon" is about a man with no life of his own who impersonates a man who, before he died, impersonated an astronaut. "A Question of Re-Entry" features a Kurtz-like character straight out of *Heart of Darkness* who tricks the Nambikwara into forming a cargo-cult devoted to an astronaut downed in the Amazon jungle.

In these stories the dead astronaut may once have been something of a hero. But those who continue to believe in the astronaut (or the glories of the late, lamented space age) are fools, even the cannibalistic Nambikwara, who eat the deified astronaut to incorporate his spirit into their bodies. The narrator of that tale tells us that what the Nambikwara are really incorporating into their former "equilibrium" with nature is the twentieth century and its "psychopathic projections." This will transform "the Indians into a community of superstitious and materialistic sightseers" (62). The easy cynicism of these stories and their total conflation of space exploration and science with the body of the dead astronaut aligns these narratives with Virilio's description of the "new romanticism of technological ruin." Ballard's stories are supposed to be about necrophilia but are themselves necrophilic, just too fascinated with those dead bodies to be able to offer any useful thinking on the impulse to venture into space, much less on the space program itself.

By contrast, Catherine Bush's 1993 novel *Minus Time* offers a brightly thoughtful meditation on the desire to go into space and on the psychical, social, and institutional ambivalences that keep women on the ground. *Minus Time* takes the individual and collective response to the *Challenger* disaster as its primal scene and then conducts a controlled experiment to try to understand every aspect of its nature and dynamic. It should not be surprising that an event like this, whose impact extended so deeply into the psyche and widely throughout the social, could best be worked through in the space of fiction. In fact, all of the criticisms I have made about NASA and all of the questions I have posed about our individual and collective difficulty in working through the meanings of the explosion and McAuliffe's death find their fictional counterpart in *Minus Time*. Thinking through this novel helped me to understand why the questions I am posing about women in space are critical and to predict where constructive answers may lie.

The novel begins with Helen, 21, and her brother Paul, 20, watching their mother being launched into space:

Their mother had left the planet. Their mother, the Canadian astronaut whom the Americans kept referring to as "one of our international astronauts," was trying along with an American astronaut to set a record for human space habitation. She had left the planet and they had no idea when she was coming back again.

For Helen, her life at that moment splits into before the launch and after. "She wanted to reach for the sky and howl out loud like a wolf—*what now*?" The rest of *Minus Time* comes to grips with that split through traveling back and forth in time— the family before the launch and the family after—to understand the reasons for and consequences of launching into space not just "a woman" but a wife, daughter, mother, teacher, and scientist. Here, we get our most developed picture yet of not only "NASA's ineptitude" and the media's drive for simplicity and sensationalism but also the social and psychic pain and ambivalence we experience around the idea of a woman going into space.

Barbara Urie, the mother in space, is a scientist who studies motion sickness. Her husband David, Helen and Paul's absent father, is concerned with the movement of the Earth's surface. A science writer turned earthquake relief worker, he has not seen his family in five years. Occasionally, he calls from Mexico City or some other tectonically active part of the world where he is busy saving others. We are never quite sure why he left, nor is he, but the likely reason is that he has never figured out how to be with a woman whose greatest desire is to leave the planet indefinitely. This is also a problem for their college-age kids, especially Helen, who seems to have little identity beyond the part of her that knows she does not want to be an astronaut like her mother. She does not want to go into space but trusts the shifting ground underneath her feet even less than her father does. Helen goes through the motions of being an anthropology student in Toronto, while her brother is more seriously studying architecture in Montreal. *Minus Time* launches these four people, this quadrangulated family, into four different spaces as part of an experiment in writing about what it means to *be* (as a person, citizen, or family) in a world made up of motion and image, where everyone is in orbit and constantly at risk of being lost in space.

The space program does not appear here as just the background for a family drama—it, too, is a family drama. All of the issues that consume families—how much closeness and how much distance is sustainable; how much trust and how much authority is needed; how much secrecy and how much disclosure is optimal—also shape the media, government, and scientific institutions that are subjects in Bush's fiction. The independent variable in this experiment is the relatively new and unevenly achieved equality of the sexes, which changes the rules and expectations for the entire range of human and social relations, everything we generally call love and work. For Helen's mother, the desire to go into space puts love and work into the sharpest possible conflict (which is apparently why Bush chose this setting for her experiment). Barbara is not only a woman in space but also a mother in space. Her children and her husband deeply do not want her to go. It is dangerous but it also hurts that she wants this more than she wants them. Still, there is no way for them to tell her that, even when she offers to let them decide whether she should go.

At the press conference called to announce her selection for the American space project, Barbara is introduced as a distinguished scientist trained in physics with a degree in medicine, a former competitive swimmer, a licensed pilot, once host of a children's TV show about science, "and on top of this, she's the mother of two children." After giving a speech about her dream of going into space, offering an impassioned defense for doing so— "like the need to survive itself, [it] is built into our genes"—and expressing her gratitude to her family for their patience, she is bombarded with reporter's questions, which only concern her decision, as a mother, to go into space. Is she proud to be the first

Canadian astronaut who is also a mother? Does she think more about the *Victory* [i.e., *Challenger*] disaster, and about the dead American astronaut who was also a mother? And finally (it gets worse): "Dr. Urie, I've read that world-class women athletes have been encouraged to have children because it seems to increase their endurance and strength. As a former competitive athlete, do you believe this?"

Shattered by the degree of self-control required for Barbara to deal with these questions (which are really accusations of being a bad mom) and by their frustration with the press, the family drives home in silence. David says softly to Barbara, "Just be glad you weren't the first person with green hair to go into space, because if you were, people would concentrate on that" (113). But, of course, the issue is of a different order: it concerns the proper role for women and challenges the very nature of femininity itself. David's protective gesture sums up the conflict for him and the children: as much as they do not want her to leave, they strongly resist the conflation of their fear of personal loss with a social demand that women's roles be restricted. What Barbara's husband and children come to understand, as does the reader, is that it is possible to feel this level of personal loss and still want your wife or mother to go into space—because she wants to and *ought* to be able to go.

Minus Time reflects on the harmful consequences of NASA's penchant for secrets and coverups by depicting the harm that occurs when the space agency's deceptions become family secrets. The book begins with Barbara Urie's launch at Cape Canaveral. Having refused to accept NASA's offer of a plane trip to Florida and a place with the astronaut families in the official viewing stands, Helen and Paul drive the 2,000 miles from Montreal to the Cape so that they can have their privacy, away from the NASA PR people and the press. Above all, they do not want to be in the viewing stands with the world's cameras trained on their faces as their mother blasts off into the sky, especially if disaster happens. ("All the families were there....They kept showing all the families screaming," Paul tells Helen later when she is recalling the day the *Victory* exploded.) After their mother has been successfully launched and as they are still trying to come to terms with the fact that she is actually in space, Helen and Paul stop at a diner on the long trip back. As the two kids watch the diner television screen replay the launch, they see themselves and their father in the viewing stands or, rather, people who look just like them:

> All three of them stared upward, mouths partly open, heads craned back toward the sky....With the roar still swelling the air around them, the other Paul and other Helen leaned toward the camera, and shouted into the microphones thrust in front of them, "We're so proud of her. It was amazing. We're incredibly proud." (12)

The real Helen and Paul are staggered by the realization that just as NASA has backup astronauts it also has backup astronaut families. Paul wonders who could have done this. Helen answers, "Networks, the American space agency, the Canadian space agency, maybe all of them, who knows?"(13). Since Helen and

Paul do not want their mother to know they were not in attendance at the official launch site, and because they think people will think they are crazy if they try to convince them such a blatant deception was staged, they decide to tell no one.

Throughout the narrative, one Urie after another feels shocked or betrayed at not having known this secret, or finding it out later than the others, or discovering that someone who promised not to tell has told. All of the activities around this secret serve only to atomize and fragment the family, eroding trust, destroying respect, engendering fear. But once everyone in the family knows the secret, it gives them a crucial bit of collective knowledge about the institutions they are caught in and a critical edge on resisting such deceptions in the future. One measure of *Minus Time*'s intelligence is that it does not argue against keeping secrets on moralistic grounds, that is, it does not argue that secrets are inherently bad. It only opposes those secrets that do damage by depriving people of the information they need to understand a situation or to move forward. But the secrets NASA keeps are precisely the kind that deprive us of information we need. It is especially invidious and hypocritical when we are deprived of information (for example, photographs of the *Challenger* crew cabin debris) in the name of protecting the dead astronauts' families.

Minus Time offers a hilarious send-up of NASA's jingoistic nationalism and its attempt to harness its frontier rhetoric project to the wagon train of national identity (again mirroring *Star Trek*, whose pitch was "*Wagon Train* to the stars"). If Helen Sharman and Arthur C. Clarke mock NASA and the U.S. through the lens of their British "let's be sensible, don't make such a fuss" attitude, Bush shows the space agency's foibles and the workings of American mythmaking through the optic of a Canadian chauvinism that is itself gently parodied. The social and psychical costs of NASA's penchant for secrets and patriotic PR and the media's taste for simplicity and sensationalism provide the contours for the narrative and characters in *Minus Time*. The novel's primal scene, then, is not so much the disaster and the death of McAuliffe as its televised representation; much of the traumatic impact came from seeing its reflection on the faces of the astronauts' families at the launch site and McAuliffe's students at her school. When the news first comes of the *Victory* disaster, Helen does not imagine the astronauts' bodies in pieces but the bodies of the astronauts' families jerking and toppling, with her mother's face over them blazing and crumbling. This gives new meaning to the term "broken families," and *Minus Time* ceaselessly deconstructs and reconstructs the implications.

The fact that Barbara is a teacher—her television show for children is called *Search for Science* and she gives lessons from the space station—identifies her even more hauntingly with McAuliffe, but it also obliquely comments on the social injunction that women should be teachers of children. Just as Sally Ride and Roberta Bondar felt they should package their experiences as astronaut-scientists in the form of children's books, the fictional Barbara, too, *must* be a teacher. It is as if women can only get the necessary social permission to acquire knowledge on condition that they do the work of processing it so that it can be retransmitted to children. There is no mention in *Minus Time* of the male American astronaut on the mission writing lesson plans or constructing visual aids with Scotch Tape and oranges, as Barbara is shown doing. By the end of the book, Barbara is able to own up to her desire to go into space to explore and do science, and to communicate that to her family. But for the rest of the world she still has to use the alibi that she is going into space for the sake of the children that she will be teaching. Male astronauts do not need the pedagogical alibi. But it is still imposed on women, or assumed by them voluntarily, if unconsciously. This is yet another of the social and psychical knots *Minus Time* offers us to reflect upon.

LOVE AND ROCKETS

How can we equate Catherine Bush's fictional launching of a woman into space with NASA putting a woman into space or the ways the media and the public construe women's participation in science and technology? How could any of the popular commentaries examined here help to reshape or substantively rewrite the currently prevailing story about women in space? This is possible because NASA has already put itself on the terrain of fiction, folklore, myth, and popular culture; NASA *is* fiction, folklore, myth, and popular culture. The entity that I earlier dubbed "NASA/TREK" is a story in the making, still in progress. All these other narratives can and do bear upon it.

Some of the pressure on NASA/TREK comes from the real world, as when Eileen Collins, the first female shuttle pilot, invited to her 1995 launch all the surviving women who had done so well on the tests for the Mercury training program in the early sixties before being dismissed by NASA precisely for having done so well. The genius of Collins's gesture lies in the way she made a bridge from NASA's typical deployment of liberal feminism—she was *the first* female shuttle pilot and carried one of Amelia Earhart's famous scarves into orbit—to a more radical feminist stance that pointedly recognized the women who should have preceded her by thirty years. As Mae Jemison put it, "Sally Ride was not the first woman to have the right stuff to go into space."[60] Collins thus went well beyond the "extraordinary woman" version of feminism to make an eloquent criticism of the political and institutional cultures that have blocked women from going into space. Collins carried with her mementoes from each of the women pilots, but the most valuable thing that she carried into space, according to one sixty two-year-old former trainee, was "our dreams and our wishes."

As we have seen, dreams and wishes about NASA and women in space appear in many forms, and the utopian urge to rewrite that story is strong and pervasive. If, indeed, *Star Trek* is the theory and NASA the practice, one would expect the TREK half of NASA/TREK to make a major contribution to writing a more inclusive and progressive story, especially since *Star Trek* aims to portray a peaceful, tolerant, nondiscriminatory culture three centuries from now. But it took seventy-eight *Star Trek* episodes, six movies, and two more television spinoff series before there was a female captain. In *Minus Time*, Helen describes the photos her mother pins to the wall, mostly of famous women scientists like Marie Curie, but also of Katharine Hepburn, who, she tells her daughter, would have made a great astronaut. In putting those words in Barbara's mouth, Catherine Bush was perhaps thinking of Hepburn's Amelia Earhart–like role as the daring and courageous pilot in Dorothy Arzner's 1933 film *Christopher Strong*. That NASA/TREK is pervaded with poetic justice can be seen in the selection of Kate Mulgrew, the spitting image (and voice) of Hepburn, to play Captain Janeway, the first female *Star Trek* captain).

Like NASA, *Star Trek* wants to foreground individual extraordinary women but not address their institutional absence, in terms of numbers or positions of authority. Women were allowed in high positions for the first time in the second *Star Trek* television series, which started in 1987 and lasted seven seasons. But even then, women were seen only in traditional caregiver roles, as the doctor and the ship's counselor. A character who crosses two of the shows, Keiko, the engineer Chief O'Brien's wife, decides to quit her job as the ship's botanist on *Next Generation*'s *Enterprise* to fashion a makeshift elementary school when she believes one is needed on *Deep Space Nine*'s space station. No one on board appears to think it odd that a research scientist would chuck her career for a lifetime with the crayon set (Chief O'Brien certainly did not volunteer). In principle, NASA and *Star Trek* should be mutually inspiring each other, pushing against each other to push forward, but instead each seems to reflect the ambivalence of the other toward the idea of women in space.

Surprisingly, some of the pressure on NASA/TREK to reconfigure how we imagine our scientific and technological future comes from NASA itself. Who could have imagined that

All female crews by 1995!

NASA BANS MEN FROM SPACE!

FEMALE RECRUIT in training for NASA's astronaut corps.

ARE MEN obsolete? Space shuttles will be manned by all-female crews by as early as 1995, experts reveal.

SALLY Ride proved that women astronauts are superior!

By BEATRICE DEXTER / *Special correspondent*

A top-secret memo leaked to the *Weekly World News* reveals that the first man on Mars is going to be a woman — because NASA plans to eliminate all male astronauts by the year 1995!

Experts at the space agency say work by French astrophysicist Joel Pilliet proves gals are far superior to guys when it comes to surviving in space. The University of Aix-Marseilles professor says a woman's temperament and physical attributes are better for long, tedious journeys outside the Earth's atmosphere, and NASA officials are so convinced by his theories they're putting them into practice.

"Women are superior to men because they can coexist for years in the cramped quarters of their spacecraft without the frustration or aggression we would see in male crews," Pilliet says.

"Their resistance to stress and tolerance for shared living will keep them in shape mentally. Their healthier bodies and greater longevity will ensure that at least some of the crew will return to Earth safely years later."

Pilliet's views, first expressed several years ago at a meeting of the European Satellite and Rocket Consortium, are now totally accepted at NASA. As a result, recruitment of female astronauts has been stepped up over the past few years and male candidates won't be accepted at all after mid-1993.

While officials at the U.S. space agency refuse to comment on their plans, sources say the ban on males is already in the works and soon only all-female crews will rocket off on missions to the stars.

"We have long known that women are in many ways stronger than men," said Pilliet when he was informed of the NASA ban. "Our species has needed women to survive to nurture the young and ensure human survival. Men are high strung and aggressive to guarantee that strong males can defend their families.

"In outer space, where a typical trip to another planet might take years, we need the quiet strength and patience of women — not the macho competition found among males.

"The American astronaut Sally Ride proves my point.

"And our studies show women to be better at the myriad small tasks entailed in life aboard a spacecraft. Women can do the job and do it right — they're so much better than men that there's no comparison."

Corpse-eating turtles!

Trained snapping turtles have been freed in India's sacred Ganges river — to clean out the thousands of partially cremated corpses floating past religious bathers.

20,000 to 30,000 cremated bodies are dumped in the river each day, along with millions of gallons of raw sewage. Religious lunatics think nothing of drinking the water they believe is so holy it can't be polluted!

Report on space science breakthrough in the *Weekly World News*.
(December 9, 1992)

CHATTER

by Kim Cunningham

UHURA HURRAH

On the recent mission of the space shuttle *Endeavour*, **Dr. Mae Jemison**, the first black woman astronaut, started her shifts by saying, "Hailing frequencies open." It was her homage to childhood hero and current pal **Nichelle Nichols**, whose interplanetary exploits (as Lieutenant Uhura on the original *Star Trek*) began in 1966. "Being able to see a black woman on the *Enterprise* exploring the heavens was very important," says Jemison, 36, who recalls this defining kindergarten conversation back home in Chicago: "I said that when I grew up I wanted to be a scientist—and the teacher asked me, 'Don't you mean a *nurse*?'"

◀ **Jemison and Nichols**

Science teams up with science fiction in *People* magazine.
(November 16, 1992)

The *Challenger* crew walks to the launchpad.
(UPI/Corbis-Bettmann)

Ten years after the *Challenger* disaster, a piece of the space shuttle washes up on a Florida beach. (Malcolm Denemark/Florida Today/Gamma Liaison)

THE 25th YEAR

The front cover of *The 25th Year* (1991). (With permission of the editor)

The back cover of *The 25th Year* (1991). (With permission of the editor)

K/S art.
(With permission of the artist)

Barbara Adams, Whitewater trial alternate juror who showed up every day dressed in full *Star Trek* uniform. (AP Photo/Danny Johnston)

one day a NASA chief would publicly berate the "pale, male, and stale" coterie at the space agency and in its related industries? In four years since his appointment in 1992, Dan Goldin has gone beyond the Dan Quayle–inspired corporate streamlining mantra "better, faster, cheaper" (criticized by some scientists for short-changing the scientific returns) to another three-part scheme more oriented toward people and science.[61] Goldin now says his job at NASA won't be finished until NASA has a more dynamic science program, until minorities and women are heavily involved in science and technology, and until the American public understands the agency's vision. He also has a flair for suturing NASA into popular culture. Perhaps his greatest stunt was arranging to fly an Oscar aboard the space shuttle *Atlantis*. During the 1992 Academy Awards ceremony, as George Lucas was being presented with the Irving G. Thalberg award for his work as a producer, his old friend Steven Spielberg directed him to look toward a vast screen. There, with the Oscar floating alongside them, was the *Atlantis* crew, live from space. The astronauts then congratulated Lucas for creating the dream of space that they were realizing.

Although Goldin is adept at using the shuttle for such popular purposes, he also knows well that the biggest stumbling block to a future NASA that would be driven by science rather than engineering or commerce and would be responsive to human, social, and environmental needs is a budget now being eaten up by the politically untouchable space shuttle and space station. To scientists, he will say what he cannot say to powerful legislators in districts that build the components for the big-ticket items. At

a 1996 meeting of the American Association for the Advancement
of Science (AAAS), Goldin said:

> I don't want to be demeaning to the people that worked on
> the shuttle, but the shuttle has suppressed a lot of science we
> could be doing. We haven't landed on a planet in 20 years
> because we've been so excited about the service support con-
> tract on the shuttle that we haven't been doing science. We
> spent 10 billion on the space station and didn't produce a
> piece of hardware, but boy did the contractors have fun. It's
> shameful. It's stealing from the American public.[62]

He went on to declare that the primary goal of planetary
exploration should be the search for present or past life forms on
other planets, and that the search should begin with robots.

But since he is probably stuck with the space shuttle (unless
space transportation becomes privatized) and the space station
(which at least offers a chance to collaborate with the Russians and
other international partners), Goldin's job will be to protect the relatively tiny science budget ($280 million for space station science
facilities out of an annual budget of $2.1 billion) that is constantly
threatened by engineering cost overruns. He must also make sure
that the new script for the Mission to Mars is one that tells the
story of sending automated sample collectors to Mars to verify
whether life exists, or existed, on another planet, in search of a scientific and philosophical answer that profoundly engages the public imagination. But there is already a rival version of the Mission
to Mars script; it exists in the minds of aerospace contractors and

in the regional newspapers where those contractors do business.

In the *Los Angeles Times*, for example, an August 1996 story with the headline "Rock May Give NASA a New Lease on Life," opened with the observation that the Mars rock had given NASA the most compelling case for space exploration since the moon landings twenty-five years ago. The article skips quickly over some of Goldin's remarks about the scientific excitement surrounding the Mars rock to quote Representative Robert S. Walker (R-Pa.), chairman of the House Science Committee, who believes that going to Mars gives new impetus to the space station program because any mission beyond Earth would require substantial research into life sciences in a zero-gravity environment. What Walker doesn't say, but which is entailed by his remark, is that the space shuttle would also have to be beefed up for such a program since the station cannot be built and serviced without it. In this Mission to Mars script, the prime purpose of following up on the Mars rock finding would be to revitalize the huge and hugely expensive industries of manned spaceflight. Goldin almost gets the last word when he says that the search for extraterrestrial life is a high road that may galvanize the public: "This is an issue of giving people something to look forward to, pulling Americans together....In the absence of an enemy, we need things greater than the Super Bowl." But the *Times* caps his remarks by saying, "And it ultimately could reinvigorate Southern California—still the world leader in space science and engineering." This gives the strong implication that going along with Walker's porkbarrelled, engineering-over-science version is what is best for the region. In fact, it's a bonanza. So much for the high road.

Here, the newspaper's regional boosterism pushes the NASA/TREK script toward a version in which the Mission to Mars is a kind of engineering Super Bowl. It is a Super Bowl in another way, too: all male except for the cheerleaders. The shuttle, the space station, and a "manned" trip to Mars are projects that are driven (like the Apollo program) almost entirely by engineering concerns. They also require military jet pilots (although this is highly debatable) to fly them or fly to them. In this scenario, science is an afterthought, allowed in only as necessary window dressing if there's enough room and funding; the same goes for women. The automated exploration missions, however, are often conceived and built in labs managed by universities, such as Caltech's Jet Propulsion Laboratory, a culture more receptive to women scientists and engineers.

Journalistic science writing plays an enormous role in the creation and ceaseless rewriting of NASA/TREK. In *Selling Science: How the Press Covers Science and Technology*, Dorothy Nelkin describes how science writing as a journalistic specialty in the U.S. took its shape from three decades of covering the space program.[63] She faults space reporters, however, for having "simply accepted what NASA fed them, reproducing the agency's assertions, promoting the prepackaged information they received, and rarely questioning the premises of the program, the competence of the scientists, or the safety of the operation" (160). But all that changed, she says, with the *Challenger* accident. That event instilled in journalists a sense of skepticism that influenced their coverage not only of space technology but of a whole range of other science and technology endeavors as well. Now, Nelkin finds, many science journalists are questioning the authority of science and asking scientists probing questions, such as "Who pays? Who is responsible? What's in it for the public? What are the stakes?" (169).

If the recent Mars rock coverage is any indication, Nelkin is right about the new critical bent. In response to NASA's "admirable caution"—putting skeptics up front even at the press conference, meticulously qualifying every finding in the published article, being quick to admit that the microfossils might be no more than dried-up mud cracks—journalists displayed their own hesitancies.[64] Nelkin says that science journalists tend to cover science only when it is "news"—that is, the breakthroughs and spectacular failures. In this case, however, the journalists communicated the barely concealed enthusiasm of the NASA scientists for what could be a major scientific breakthrough, while trying to give it a social and historical context. They consistently included the voices of the skeptics and NASA's most stalwart critics of the agency's lack of a clearly articulated scientific mission. Newspaper editors, too, made sure to embed the coverage of the Mars rock findings in discussions of the religious and philosophical implications of discovering life on another planet. It remains to be seen, however, to what extent the newly critical science journalism will contribute to the version of NASA/TREK I would like to see take shape, given the kind of political and economic priorities so insistently promoted in the *Los Angeles Times* article.

I have considered a long line of people, practices, and institutions that have more and less successfully contributed to rewriting NASA/TREK. This long line includes ordinary people such as Christa McAuliffe's mother, Grace Corrigan, as well as

NASA scientists, such as Eric Chaisson, who has strongly articulated the space agency's failure to communicate its vision to scientists, the media, and ordinary people, and Yvonne Clearwater, the environmental psychologist who risked her position to argue for investigating issues of sex and sexuality on long-term space missions (even when told that in her studies she was to assume that "sex simply would not occur").[65] Former astronaut Sally Ride significantly rewrote NASA/TREK by offering the first elaboration of Mission to Planet Earth when she insisted on the necessity of obtaining a comprehensive scientific understanding of the entire Earth System, in her 1987 report *Leadership and America's Future in Space*. Current astronaut Eileen Collins, as we saw, made the most eloquent and explicitly feminist criticism of NASA yet for its history of resistance to launching qualified women into space. And British cosmonaut Helen Sharman (with a tip of the hat from Arthur C. Clarke) gave us a witty, no-nonsense view of a woman's efforts to negotiate space agency PR and media mania to make her own place in space. In *Minus Time* Catherine Bush provides an especially strong fictional girl side to the reigning boy narrative—the fire-on-the-moon of Norman Mailer, the "right stuff" of Tom Wolfe, and the nostalgic necrologies of J.G. Ballard.

But perhaps the most radical rewriting of NASA/TREK has occurred underground, even below the grassroots. It is now time to look at how NASA/TREK got slashed.

/TREK

Popular scientists can be found just about anywhere, if we only know how to recognize them. *Star Trek* fans, of course, are popular scientists in both their fictional and real-world commitments.[66] They sustain an enormous interest in the space program and are conscientious about following its development, its failures, and the vicissitudes of its funding. Perhaps contrary to expectation, the fans do not overwhelmingly support the manned space program and are just as skeptical as most people, if not more so, about the scientific payoffs of the space shuttle and the space station. In fact, *Star Trek* fans may be among the readiest to forgo expensive manned space voyages until automated explorations have first gained as much knowledge as possible. After all, these fans have the richly detailed fictional space travel of *Star Trek* and all its spinoffs to tide them over until humans return to the moon or travel to the red planet and beyond.

Not surprisingly, the *Challenger* disaster devastated *Star Trek* fans. They responded with filksongs (fan folksongs) and stories to try to come to terms with the loss. In one novel-length work of fan fiction, the author rewrote NASA's choice of Christa McAuliffe to be the first civilian in space by having NASA instead select actor Nichelle Nichols (Lt. Uhura) to go up on the *Challenger*, in appreciation of her work for the space agency recruiting women and minority astronaut candidates. Perhaps the writer felt that Nichols' death would make more sense given her greater length of involvement with NASA, her superior professionalism, and her noncivilian status, at least in her role as the *Enterprise* communications officer.

Many *Star Trek* fans believe that their experience with extrapolatory fiction has given them a privileged ability to "think global" and to be concerned with environmental issues. They see themselves as firmly committed to a politics of equality and tolerance, devoted as they are to a rather sunny version of Kennedy-era liberalism, as reinterpreted through the Vulcan philosophy of IDIC, Infinite Diversity in Infinite Combinations. This particular spin on Camelot neglects the Kennedy of the Bay of Pigs and the attempted CIA assassinations of world leaders in favor of the Kennedy of civil rights, the Peace Corps, and a farsighted space program.

So, too, the fans' anti-imperialist leanings, based on their respect for the Federation's Prime Directive of noninterference in "developing" cultures, can be as shaky and inconsistent as they ever were on *Star Trek*. Although fans delight in keeping a tally of the number of times the Prime Directive has been broken—so many times, in fact, that it has become the exception rather than the rule—their own tendency toward anti-imperialism is undermined in the same way the Prime Directive is undermined in the *Star Trek* universe: in the original show (and its successor) it is never clear whether the *Enterprise* was on a scientific or military mission. Furthermore, if the *Enterprise* is a United Federation of Planets starship, why is it called the *U.S.S. Enterprise*? In the original *Star Trek*, its successor *Star Trek: The Next Generation*, and the fandom itself, a preference for peaceful uses of technology and the principle of noninterference can exist side by side with nationalistic patriotism and unrestrained affection for militarist uses of technology. A Trekker can thus, without apparent contradiction, adopt the precepts of IDIC, the Prime Directive, and the peaceful use of technology while still exulting in the American "victory" in Grenada or enthusiastically supporting Star Wars/SDI. But, in the main, most Trekkers use those precepts to create or undergird a liberal humanistic or left libertarian ideology.

Trek fandom also shows its commitments in its social constituency. It is interracial, includes people of all ages, has a fair number of disabled members, is sexually balanced, and has a strong cross-class representation, though perhaps most members are in the pink-collar, "subprofessional," or high-tech service industry sectors. This is not to say that *Trek* fandom is incapable of self-contradiction, discrimination, bad politics, bad faith, and all the rest. But this huge base of fans (35,000 official fan-club members, with many thousands more in smaller, unofficial clubs, or unaffiliated) represents one of the most important populist sites for debating issues of the human and everyday relation to science and technology. This is why *Star Trek* fandom has been so important to the creation of NASA/TREK. But the specific group of fans that I want to discuss here is a much smaller segment of *Star Trek* fandom as a whole. It is made up of several hundred women who inhabit a subculture that exists within and alongside the larger, and far more legitimate, fandom. These women are responsible for the most radical rewriting of NASA/TREK yet.

" / "

Near the end of *Star Trek V: The Final Frontier*, Captain Kirk, thought to be dead but rescued finally by Spock and some exceptionally helpful Klingons, stands facing his first officer on the bridge of the Klingon ship. Glad to be alive, he moves toward Spock and reaches for him with both hands. Spock interrupts the embrace saying, "Please, Captain, not in front of the Klingons." Kirk directs a brief glance toward the known universe's most macho aliens, then turns back to Spock to exchange a complicitous look before lowering his hands. Most members of the audience probably took this teasing one-liner as just another instance of what actor and director William Shatner has called the "tongue-in-cheek" campiness of the original TV series.[67]

But for a small minority of the audience, a group of female fans who have for years dedicated themselves to writing and publishing underground pornographic stories about Kirk and Spock as spacefaring lovers, this scene came as a delightful surprise. Moreover, it seemed to be an astonishing recognition of their fantasies by a *Star Trek* industry that has up until now met those desires with curt dismissals, cute evasions, or disdainful silence.[68] It is not yet clear what it will mean for these fans to have had their desires recognized and their fantasies ratified, not only by Shatner but, indirectly, by the Great Bird of the Galaxy, *Star Trek* creator Gene Roddenberry. It may be that these fans will feel some erosion of the pleasure that comes from its secret, marginalized solidarity. In the past, they have gained particular delight in seeing how their guerrilla erotics shocked and enraged (and, surely, sometimes amused) the producers of *Star Trek*, as well as other fans involved in more official *Star Trek* fandom, and "mundanes" (as they call nonfans) who may have stumbled across some of the steamier stories in fanzines like *Naked Times*, *Off Duty*, *Fever*, and *Final Frontier*. What is more likely, however, is that this fleeting public recognition of their hitherto illicit desires will only spur them on. The group solidarity of these fans rests not only on the taboo nature of their work but also on their pride in having created a unique, hybridized genre that ingeniously blends romance, pornography, and utopian science fiction. They are also fiercely proud of having created a comfortable yet stimulating social space in which women can manipulate the products of mass-produced culture to stage a popular debate around issues of technology, fantasy, and everyday life. This, of course, is my version of it, based on a decade of familiarity with their work. The fans (who refer to me as "one of the academic fans") would say they are just having fun.

Women have been writing *Star Trek* pornography for at least twenty years, mostly in the United States, but also in Britain, Canada, and Australia. The idea did not begin with one person who then spread it to others, but seems to have arisen spontaneously in various places beginning in the early to mid-seventies. Through seeing the episodes countless times in syndication and on their own taped copies, these fans recognized that there was an erotic homosexual subtext there, or at least one that could easily be *made* to be there. Most of the writers and readers started off in "regular" *Star Trek* fandom, and many are still involved in it, even while they pursue their myriad activities in what is called "K/S" or "slash" fandom. To those purchasing amateur fanzines (or "zines") by mail, the slash between K(irk) and S(pock) serves as a code indicating that the stories, poems, and artwork published there concern a same-sex relationship between the two men. Such a designation stands in contrast to "ST" (with no slash), for example, which identifies action-adventure stories fans write based on the *Star Trek* fictional universe, or "adult ST," which refers to stories containing sexual scenes, but heterosexual ones only, say between Captain Kirk and Lt. Uhura or between Spock and Nurse Chapel.

Other media male couples have been "slashed" in the zines, such as Starsky and Hutch (S/H), Simon and Simon (S/S), *Miami Vice*'s Crockett and Castillo (M/V) or, more recently, *Wise Guy*'s Vinnie and McPike (W/G). The slash premise, however, seems to work exceptionally well with science fiction couples because of all the possibilities opened up by locating the two men in a futuristic universe full of scientific and technological wizardry. K/S was the first slash writing, and it dominated the field for many years; its first real rival was a newer science fiction fandom based on *Blake's 7*, a British television show broadcast from 1978 to 1981. As we shall see, the popularity and success of SF slash are due to the range and complexity of discourses that are possible in a genre that could be described as romantic pornography radically shaped and reworked by the themes and tropes of science fiction.

The conventions of the science fiction genre seem to offer several important advantages to the writing of "pornography by women, for women, with love" (as Joanna Russ once described slash writing).[69] It has been argued that science fiction, seemingly the most sexless of genres, is in fact engrossed with questions of sexual difference and sexual relations, which it repeatedly addresses alongside questions of other kinds of differences and relations: humans and aliens, humans and machines, time travelers and those they visit, and so on.[70] In *Feminism and Science Fiction*, Sarah Lefanu has argued that science fiction offers women writers a freedom not available in mainstream writing. This is because its generic form—with its overlooked roots in the female gothic novel and nineteenth-century feminist utopian literature—permits a fusing of political concerns with the "playful creativity of the imagination."[71] And this is so, she says, even though science fiction has historically been a male preserve.

Lefanu limits herself, however, to rounding up the usual suspects, those women science fiction writers with self-conscious feminist politics who have written stories and novels that have, nonetheless, been able to make it into the SF mainstream. Those writers include such well-known figures as Ursula Le Guin, Joanna Russ, Suzy McKee Charnas, and James Tiptree, Jr. (Alice Sheldon), as well as feminist writers in the literary mainstream, like Marge Piercy and Margaret Atwood, who have on occasion made use of SF themes and tropes. Lefanu's focus on professional women writers with self-conscious feminist politics is one shared by the major critics of female SF, Frances Bartkowski, Anne Cranny-Francis, and Marleen S. Barr. Barr's project, for example, is to distance female SF as far as possible from its roots in popular genre fiction by relabeling it "feminist fabulation" and arguing for its place at the center of experimental postmodern fiction.

The women writers I want to discuss, however, are amateur writers who embrace the popular culture of television. They are generally unwilling to identify themselves as feminists, even though their writing and their fan activity might seem to offer an indirect (and sometimes not so indirect) commentary on issues usually seen as feminist, such as women's lack of social and economic equality, their having to manage a double-duty work and domestic life, and their being held to much greater standards of physical beauty than men.

Historian and cultural anthropologist Michel de Certeau once used the term "Brownian motion" to describe the tactical maneuvers of the relatively powerless when attempting to resist, negotiate, or transform the system and products of the relatively powerful.[72] He defined *tactics* as guerrilla actions involving hit-and-run acts of apparent randomness. Tactics are not designed primarily to help users take over the system but to allow them to seize every opportunity to convert to their own ends forces that systematically exclude or marginalize them. These tactics are also *a way of thinking* and "show the extent to which intelligence is inseparable from the everyday struggles and pleasures that it articulates."[73] The only "product" of such tactics is one that results from "making do," the *bricolage* process of combining already existing heterogeneous elements. It is not a synthesis that takes the form of an intellectual discourse about an object; the form of its making is its intelligence. The K/S fans, however, seem to go de Certeau's "ordinary man" one better. They are not just reading, viewing, or consuming in tactical ways that offer fleeting moments of resistance or pleasure while watching TV, scanning the tabloids, or selecting from the supermarket shelves (to take some of his examples). They are producing not just intermittent, cobbled-together acts but real products — zines, novels, artworks, and videos. These products mimic and mock those of the industry they are "borrowing" from while offering pleasures found lacking in the originals.

Slash fandom more than illustrates de Certeau's claim that consumption is itself a form of production. A mini-industry, but one that necessarily makes no money (the only thing saving it from copyright suits), it has its own apparatuses of advertising and publishing; juried prizes (K/Star, Surak, and Federation Class of Excellence Awards); stars (the top editors, writers, and artists, but also fans who have become celebrities); house organ, *On the Double*; annual meetings, featuring charity fund-raisers (for example, art auctions to support pediatric AIDS research or earthquake relief); music videos (with scenes from *Star Trek* reedited for their "slash" meanings); brilliant built-in market research techniques (the consumers are the producers and vice versa, since many of the slash readers are also its writers); and, increasingly, the elements of a critical apparatus, with its own theorists and historians.[74] The fandom has achieved a form of vertical integration — control over every aspect of production, distribution, and consumption — that the trust-busted film industry could only dream about until Reagan-Bush deregulation began to make it possible again.

Although this fan publishing apparatus could not exist without the prior existence of the *Star Trek* industry, its relation to that industry cannot be described as parasitic. Parasites generally injure or sap their hosts, but slash fandom in no way seeks to harm or destroy the world of *Star Trek*, even the often unsatisfying version presented in the second television series, *Star Trek: The Next Generation* (1987–94), whose cold, high-tech surfaces, straightlaced characters, and lack of humor have made it relatively impervious to slashing. Rather, the fans only want to *use* the system imposed by the other, a practice that, as de Certeau describes it, "redistributes its space; it creates at least a certain play in that order, a space for maneuvers of unequal forces and for utopian points of reference." This is where, he says, one discovers the "opacity" of popular culture:

> a dark rock that resists all assimilation....the subtle, stubborn, resistant activity of groups which, since they lack their own space, have to get along in a network of already established forces and representations. People have to make do with what they have....We see the tactical and joyful dexterity of the mastery of a technique.[75]

In many ways, however, slash fans do more than "make do"; they make. Not only have they remade the *Star Trek* fictional universe to their own desiring ends, they have accomplished this by enthusiastically mimicking the technologies of mass-market cultural production and by constantly debating their own relation, as women, to those technologies. They have, therefore, carefully considered the ways they make decisions about how to use the technological resources available to them and the ways they rewrite bodies and technologies in their utopian romances.

APPROPRIATE TECHNOLOGY

The term "appropriate technology" (borrowed from green criticism) refers to both everyday uses of technology that are appropriate to the job at hand and the way users decide how and what to appropriate. To avoid becoming dependent on sources that extract too high a price, or to ensure that the technology will be available to everyone, one appropriates only what is needed. The slashers (their name for themselves) are constantly involved in negotiating appropriate levels of technology for use within the fandom. The emphasis is on keeping the technology accessible and democratic, although this turns out to be easier said than done. The general perception among fans is that media zine editors give more attention to the appearance of their publications than do SF literature zine editors, and that overall they look a lot slicker—laser-printed and xeroxed rather than mimeoed, for example. And it is true that the media zines, and especially the slash zines, look very good. They are beautifully produced, with glossy, illustrated covers; spiral, velo, or even perfect bindings; color xerography on the cover or inside; laser-printed type; and intricate page borders.

However, given the high level of everyday technological skills the fans must have developed in their jobs as nurses, teachers, office workers, librarians, copy shop managers, and so on, what is striking is that the zines, as good as they look, are not as slick as they could be. In part, this may arise from an impulse to keep them looking *slightly* tacky to give them that illegitimate pornographic cast. One of the binding forces of slash fan culture is the shared delight in the visual shock value of the zines. Although zine publishers claim that they cannot afford heavy-duty plain envelopes for mailing, I have often suspected that an important element of this fandom's pleasure lies in the illicit thrill of receiving in the mail—to the stares and smiles of one's mail carrier, friends, family, or colleagues—a half-torn envelope revealing a particularly juicy drawing of Kirk and Spock, their naked bodies arranged in some near-impossible position. (This has happened to me.) But it is more likely that the publishing technology is only semi-developed because deliberate decisions have been made to keep the technology "appropriate," unintimidating, accessible, and hence democratic.

Workshops on the "how-to" of zine publishing are offered at each convention, and the zine editors who run the workshops are generous with their advice, sharing what they have learned from experience. Several helpful pamphlets, also full of advice, with step-by-step instructions on how to edit and publish a zine, are available from fan editors. One zine editor/publisher who works at a copy center put out a brochure advertising its services in this way:

> I am sure you are aware of the increasingly high cost of copying and binding and the difficulty in finding a printer who is quality-minded, reliable, economical and gives the confidentiality that your publications deserve. If you have missed

deadlines, encountered poor printing quality and/or disapproving counter personnel, then look no further for a remedy — CopyMat can save the day.

Occasionally, however, there will be a fan revolt against even this apparently easy and democratic access to new publishing technologies. Many of the female fans of *The Professionals* (a British secret service show), one of the strongest non-SF slash alternatives to K/S, have almost entirely eschewed zine publishing in favor of what is called "circuit fandom." If a fan wants to read the latest *Professionals* stories, she sends a stamped, self-addressed envelope to a designated fan in Illinois, who sends out ten of the most recently received stories. Or, if she is a new fan, she can ask the fan who manages the circuit to pick out the "ten best" stories to send to her. The fan does her own photocopying and sends the originals back to Illinois. *Professionals* stories are often not advertised, edited, or even "published," but are simply disseminated in the most basic way imaginable, among fans who say they are fed up with what they see as the technological hassles of zine publishing, its ridiculously high standards for copyediting and illustration, and its resultant overprofessionalization. They also object to the "difficult" personalities of some zine editors, by which they mean editors who publish only themselves and their friends or who censor certain kinds of stories.[76]

The issue of observing appropriate levels of technology is a contested one for the fans. Fan editors who are skilled with, have access to, and are unable to resist the lure of the latest technology ("Take advantage of CopyMat's Canon Laser Color Copier") often wish to produce ever more sophisticated looking zines. On the other hand, fan readers are often suspicious of this tendency toward more professional looking publications, feeling that the "look" of the zine is entirely secondary to the content of the stories and the quality of the writing. And fan writers object when they feel that editors are spending less time copyediting and proofreading their work than soliciting work from fan artists and perfecting their graphics technology. Complicating this debate even further is the fact that there are no clear divisions among readers, writers, artists, and editor/publishers, and therefore no correspondingly clear conflicts among their respective interests. Almost all fan readers are also writers, many are editors of their own zines, and some are also artists; some of the most enduring and prolific editor/publishers also perform all the other roles. Conflicting impulses, then, about appropriate levels of technology can be harbored by a single person. But all of the fans, no matter how much some of them might feel pulled toward a greater "professionalism," still voice the shared desire to keep the technology of the publishing apparatus within the reach of all.

Just as the fans are split over the uses of technology, they also have conflicting desires about amateur versus professional levels of writing. They are militant in their desire to maintain an unintimidating milieu in which women who want to write can do so without fear of being held to external, professional standards of "good writing." The pride and pleasure the fans take in their writing is immense. They talk about it as a form of escape from the pressures of their daily domestic and work lives; they see it as superior to the more passive escape provided by romance reading, for example. But they value writing even more for the expression of individual creativity it allows. Above all, they recognize that they feel free to express themselves as writers only insofar as they can conceive of their writing as a hobby and nothing more. Even this commitment to thinking of what they do as a hobby, however, gets subtly subverted by the fans themselves. At the most basic level of standards of punctuation and typographical accuracy, for example, fans demand that writers and editors be meticulous in catching and correcting errors. Such errors, they claim, can break the erotic fantasy when they occur at important moments in the story. There are fan editors, of course, who defend themselves by saying that they would rather spend their time finding good stories than nitpicking over every typo and misspelling. But in general everyone prefers errorless stories.

The strong pull toward "professionalization" is described by the fans in terms of getting "hooked" or "contaminated" by the writing and editing process. One fan writer and editor came up with what she calls "the virus theory of fandom":

reading = contact

writing = infection

editing = full-blown disease

The virus theory of fandom attempts to account for the tendency to become fascinated and then obsessed with the craft of writing, to want to delve ever deeper into its techniques to produce something that pleases both the author and the readers. As two fan editors remarked during a slash convention writing panel, "Fans go in because they need to create something and then feel good when it goes out and others like it." Another possible motive for wanting to write, and write well, was voiced by a third editor on this panel: "It also makes you feel that you're not abnormal for having picked up on the relationship between Starsky and Hutch!"

The most palpable tension between the commitment to amateurism and the wish to perfect one's craft along more professional lines can be seen in the popular writing panel discussions and workshops offered at every slash convention. Although the fans want to learn all they can from the more experienced writers leading the discussion, they often tend to resist workshop leaders' emphasis on technique and craft in favor of a focus on inspiration and the "magic" of writing. And in response to a long series of specific suggestions by one experienced fan writer about how to fashion a story idea as effectively as possible, another fan objected by insisting (albeit rather plaintively), "There's a place for stuff that's just so-so." But perhaps the greatest source of tension lies in the fans' knowledge of how many of their cohorts have "crossed over" into professional writing. Many of these writers (indeed, most of them) maintain their relation to fandom because they still want to be part of that supportive community, and they feel very loyal to it, even when they have become successful in commercial writing. One of America's most respected female science fiction writers, who has more than dabbled in slash writing (and who wishes to go unnamed), told poet and novelist Marge Piercy, who told me, "Forget Breadloaf. Forget the Iowa Writers Workshop. Slash fandom is the best writing workshop in the country."

Many of the fans show visible pride in fellow slash writers who have gone pro, even those who have done so by deslashing and heterosexualizing their own or others' work to turn it into commercial stories or novels. (Some of the *Star Trek* paperback novels are based on slash stories or were written by slash writers.) But their ambivalence, which is, I think, finally productive, still manifests itself. At a slash convention panel discussion on precisely this topic, one fan commented, "It's not our best writers who've gone pro." Another fan scoffed, "That's what we like to think!" I call it a productive ambivalence because it is one that impels the fans to debate not simply the merits of "amateur" versus "pro" writing. They must also address the assumptions shaping those categories, and do so by challenging the idea that only those who are already "credentialed" may be allowed access to the means of acquiring cultural capital through writing fiction or poetry.

The fans seem less concerned about their relation to video technologies than they are to writing technologies. Although the video contest is often the high point of a slash convention, going on for a tremendously raucous and pleasurable three or four hours, fewer of the fans are involved in making videos, or "songtapes," as they are called. One reason is obvious: the greater difficulty of access to video equipment, especially editing equipment, than to desktop publishing and photocopying technologies, which are often available in the fan's own workplace and can be used even while on the job. That the fans are concerned to make this technology more available, however, can be seen in the scheduling at fan conventions of workshops such as one I attended called "Song Tapes for the Masses." The workshop, organized by two fan video artists known for making songtapes that are not particularly slick but highly effective and popular with the fans, offered the novice or would-be songtape producer advice that was both practical and aesthetic. The songtapes are, in fact, music videos made right at home with two VCRs, an audio cassette deck, and a stopwatch. The organizers of the workshop handed out a helpful chart that allows the songtape maker to write down each line of, usually, a rock song with a love theme, the duration of each phrase, and the duration of the video segment that will be matched with it. The video segments are taken from fans' private collections of the seventy-eight (plus the pilot) *Star Trek* episodes and the seven *Star Trek* films, which are also on tape, copied from video store rentals.

The K/S video artist begins by cataloguing all the scenes of Kirk and Spock together, and then selects the ones that when matched with the music will bring out what the fans call the "slash premise," that is, that the two men are in love and sexually involved with each other. As I said before, the advice ranges from the practical ("Look at your video material without sound — the sound will confuse you"; "Use the show's own cuts, fades, dissolves, etc. since you can't do them yourself") to the aesthetic ("Watch MTV or VH1 and just see what they do"; "Don't be too literal, for example, having a line like 'rain is pouring down' and showing someone in the shower").

What was stressed throughout the workshop was keeping the production as cheap as possible ("Time the song segments with a $5.00 stopwatch") and the built-in advantages of lo-tech ("Hi-fi isn't important since it will come out mono on most machines anyway"). However, as the workshop progressed, the organizers, who have been making songtapes for many years, could not resist telling us about some of the neat things they have learned to do with this basic equipment and demonstrating a few of their shortcuts through what is admittedly a tedious and labor-intensive process. The discussion began to get increasingly more technical, involving editing processes that would require additional, and relatively more expensive, equipment. For example, they suggested that everyone get a video insert machine ("no roll-back") and a machine with a flying advance head ("no jittery shots or rainbows"). And, finally, at the very end of the work-shop: "Really, what you should do is buy an editing machine." They recommended the Panasonic lap editor from Radio Shack for $147.00, a price that would be out of the range of many of the novice songtape producers. Still, the advice was so clear and the directions so explicit that one came away from the workshop not feeling intimidated by the apparatus but rather that one could adopt whatever level of technology one felt able to handle and could afford.

One piece of technology about which the fans have no ambivalence whatever is the VCR, which, along with zine publishing machinery, is the lifeblood of the fandom. The ubiquitous VCR allows fans to copy episodes for swapping or for closer examination of their slash possibilities, and provides the basic technology for producing songtapes. Fans are deeply invested in VCR technology because it is cheap, widely available, easy to use, and provides both escape and a chance to criticize the sexual status quo. As one beautifully embroidered sampler at a fan art auction put it, "The more I see of men, the more I love my VCR."

Slash fandom's move onto the Internet was as carefully and

thoughtfully negotiated as its step up to other newer, more advanced technologies. At a fan convention I attended in 1996, about forty women met to discuss the impact of the Internet on slash writing and the fan community. All but two of the women were already active in fan culture on the Internet. The on-line fans spoke glowingly of the possibilities the Internet offered for sharing writing and ideas but expressed some ambivalence about slash becoming more widely known if this brought the risk of diluting the fandom. They also evinced concern over the risk of erosion of community if electronic communication ever came to substitute for face-to-face contact. The majority of the fans in the room were enthusiastic yet thoughtfully cautious about the new Internet fan culture. The two women who were not yet on the Internet were far less enthusiastic about the move into cyberspace. They expressed resentment over the cost of joining fan culture on the Internet and said they felt intimidated by its technological complexity. In typical slash fashion, by the end of the hour-long discussion, the holdouts had been humorously cajoled and mentored into a promise to give the Internet a try.

SLASH TACTICS: TECHNOLOGIES OF WRITING

Just as slash fans are constantly debating and negotiating their relation to technology within the fandom, so does this concern appear in the fictions of the stories they write. In one way, the fans' task of writing stories involving science and technology has been made easier for them. For such an elaborately produced science fiction show (even though much of it looks hokey to us now), the original *Star Trek* had a curiously ambivalent relation to the representation of futuristic technology. Although the producers of the show consulted scientists, engineers, and technicians in their efforts to make the science and technology plausible, they decided finally to give only the barest and sketchiest of outlines, to keep, for example, the design of the ship and the various scientific, medical, and military instruments extremely basic and simple. Not only was this decision an economical one (for example, some of Dr. McCoy's medical instruments were made from saltshakers), simplicity helped to ensure that the technology would not quickly look dated. "Phasers," "tricorders," "communicators," "scanners," "photon torpedoes," and "warp drive" were therefore designed to reveal their functions without divulging anything about how they were actually supposed to work. Franz Joseph's *Star Fleet Technical Manual*, first published in 1975, promises on its cover that one will find inside "detailed schematics of Star Fleet equipment," "navigational charts and equipment," and "interstellar space/warp technology," but fails to deliver anything but exhaustive descriptions of the way the instruments *look*, saying nothing of their functioning or theoretical basis.[77]

While some fans have felt compelled to flesh out the sketchy contours of *Star Trek* science and technology, they have mostly been men. For example, an ad in an issue of *Datazine* for a zine called *Sensor Readings*, edited by Bill Hupe, says that it "features articles on warp factor cubed theory (by Tim Farley), shuttlecraft landing approach methods (by Steven K. Dixon), [and] the electronic printing methods available to fanzine editors today (by Randall Landers, a former Kinko's manager)." This is not to say that male *Star Trek* fans, who are more likely to edit the nonfiction zines, invariably exhibit a more developed relation to high technology than do women fans, who form the great majority of fiction zine writers and publishers. Rather, what I want to emphasize is that the women *Star Trek* fans, especially the slash fans, have defined *technology* in a way that includes the technologies of the body, the mind, and everyday life. It is a notion of technology that sees everything in the world (and out of this world) as interrelated and subject to influence by more utopian and imaginative desires than those embodied in existing technological hardware.

This is the way Alexis Fegan Black, one of the most prolific K/S writers and publishers, suggests that aspiring slash writers approach the question of technology:

> Perhaps most importantly, WRITE WHAT YOU KNOW! That isn't to say that you can't write about being on board the *Enterprise* because you obviously have never been there. But if you *are* going to write a story that deals in mechanical or electronic details with the workings of the *Enterprise*, do so convincingly. A good rule of thumb is that it's best *not* to use what sci-fi writers call "pseudo-science" (cursory explanations of something dredged up solely from imagination) unless absolutely necessary.

But Black tells slash writers to take heart:

> Fortunately, the K/S genre is one wherein technology can usually be kept to a minimum. And writing what you know

should be on a more emotional level than a technological one in most cases.

She goes on to say that she herself has been able to take up subjects like martial arts, cryogenics, and metaphysics because she has already researched those areas and thus the effort to come up with convincing detail does not take away from attention to the "emotional" aspects of the story. Black describes her own writing as "technomysticism," and even though her work is more directly inspired by New Age ideas than most slash writing, it is instructive for understanding the genre's relation to technology to see how this extremely influential writer (she has written more K/S novels than any other slash writer and manages the largest K/S press) folds descriptions of outer space into meditations on inner space.

Science fiction writing is usually broken down into two schools: so-called hard SF (men and machines colonizing the galaxies) and soft SF (work that extrapolates from ideas found in the human and social sciences, like sociology, psychology, or anthropology, rather than the natural or physical sciences). There are, of course, countless examples of blurred boundaries and crossovers (and increasingly so), but work like Black's would seem at first sight firmly ensconced in the soft school. Her work, however, does not read like, say, that of Ursula Le Guin, the avatar of SF based in the human and social sciences, and indeed Black's references are not to any disciplines recognized by the academy but to more popular ones derived from "pop" psychology, New Age ideas, the environmental movement, and a peculiarly American brand of libertarianism that believes itself to be the inheritor of Kennedy-era liberalism.

A closer look at Black's most well-received novel, *Dreams of the Sleepers*, the first in a trilogy of fan award-winning books, will give a sense of what she means by "technomysticism." Published in 1985, *Dreams of the Sleepers* is a time-travel story, which, like most such stories, revels in the dizzying paradoxes of journeying through time. The zine/book begins with an editorial titled "What's It All About?" We are plunged into a narrative in which four men in black arrive at the author's home in vans with government license plates. Her home is next to a "missile testing range" that she is sure is really a government installation for detaining captured aliens. They want to know how she found out about Kirk and Spock, and say that they would like "to ask...a few questions about this manuscript....What's this all about?" This little narrative turns into a proper editorial in which the author says that *Dreams of the Sleepers* aims to get the reader to ask the crucial question, "What *would* this world be like without *Star Trek*?"

We are then returned to the narrative, in which Alexis finds what she takes to be a prank letter under her door, a letter from Dr. McCoy to Admiral Nogura of Star Fleet Command. The letter accompanies a manuscript that McCoy claims he confiscated during the *Enterprise* crew's continuing mission into Earth's past, while they wait for Kirk and Spock's return, the two having inexplicably disappeared. Now the novel itself begins, with an entry in the captain's log: the crew has been ordered on a mission into Earth's past, to the year 1963, to be precise. Their mission is to find out everything they can about old Earth's early experimentation with "psychotronics," the psychic manipulation of reality. Meanwhile, Kirk and Spock are feeling the first stirrings of what they are slowly realizing is their love and passion for one another, although their relationship has not yet been consummated, and each man does not yet know the depth of the other man's feelings. Just before beaming down to Earth, Spock suggests that he and Kirk form a mind link "for security reasons" while on their mission (as a half-Vulcan, Spock has the ability to link up with another mind empathically and even telepathically). Through the link, Kirk and Spock understand for the first time that their desire is mutual.

Almost immediately after beaming down to the military/scientific installation, which turns out to be the private but government-funded Futura Technics, Kirk and Spock are captured and put into life suspension units, but not before they learn the purpose of the project. Scientists have been lured to Futura Technics to work on life suspension for space exploration, but soon find out that the project's real aim is to harness the psychic energy of the "sleepers" for use as defensive and offensive weapons, as well as sabotage of all kinds. Humans have been captured and suspended, and aliens, too. Indeed, a Klingon sleeper is slated to travel out of his body on the next mission, two days hence—the assassination of John F. Kennedy! (Oliver Stone, take note.) The head of the project explains to Kirk and Spock, before putting them under, that certain people in the government and military fear Kennedy's popularity and believe that if he lives, the country will become truly united and could then be led into peace, not war. But the Futura Technics scientists do not want peace to come so soon, and certainly not on Kennedy's terms. They also want "peace," but only after conquering the rest of the world with their psychotronic weapons—the dreams of the sleepers. They will kill people by making them *believe* they have been attacked by nuclear weapons.

After Kirk and Spock are put to "sleep" in life suspension units, it is Spock who first awakes into his astral form. Another astral traveler who is also a sleeper in the complex teaches Spock how to move around in space but also in time. He takes Spock twenty-two years into the future to show him a world devastated by war and hints to him that the end of the world is somehow linked to something Spock and Kirk either did or did not do. Kirk finally awakes into his astral body and joins Spock, eventually setting up housekeeping on the astral plane; finding a nicely decorated and uninhabited ranch house nearby, they "move in" and begin to pass the time with elaborate sexual fantasies and lovemaking (a prescient description of virtual reality cybersex).

Spock takes Kirk forward twenty-two years to see the postapocalyptic ruin of the planet. Kirk weeps for all the dead but also, more selfishly, for himself, because if this future comes to pass, he will never have been born and he and Spock will never be able to join together as friends, lovers, or the twin souls they have now become. Suddenly, they notice that another man has materialized, sitting cross-legged under a tree. The man shakes hands with Spock, then laughs with joy and disbelief. "I *knew* it!...Damn! I knew it....You're *real*." "Gene," the man under the tree, is, of course, Gene Roddenberry. Spock immediately recognizes him as the key to changing the future: if this "strange messiah in polyester leisure-wear" can only realize his dream for all to see—of a populous and peace-loving federation of all the galaxies' creatures—then humans will be inspired to give up waging war on each other and go to the stars instead.

To help Roddenberry realize his dream, Spock links his mind with Gene's to show him the future. Spock decides that this is the "logical" thing to do, even though Gene will also see his most private thoughts and will understand the nature of his relationship with Kirk. But coming out in this fashion is "a fair price to purchase a world's survival." Gene promises that in return he will find some way to help rescue them from the complex. Thus: "On September 8, 1966 [the date the first episode of *Star Trek* was broadcast], the future formed a tentative bond with the present, interlinking its parts with the past. After three years, however, that link was severed. But throughout the world, minds were altered in subtle ways." Underachievers and autistic children begin functioning brilliantly. Technology is turned to peaceful purposes. Educational levels rise dramatically and knowledge is no longer the property of the elite. Advanced computers become available to everyone. Peace breaks out all over. The space program expands, transforming science fiction into fact, and the first space shuttle is named *Enterprise* by popular acclaim (which, as we saw, actually happened). Meanwhile, Kirk and Spock dream on, not knowing about the new world they have helped to create, and not knowing when or if their liberator will ever come. They again travel into the future, but this time apocalypse has been avoided. Gene appears, saying maybe he's just an idealist but he'd like to think that they had something to do with it. And he shows

Kirk and Spock episodes of *Star Trek*, telling them how influential the show has been, how many followers it has had, and so on.

In talking about *Star Trek* later, Kirk says to Spock that Gene was wrong about one thing: "Space isn't the final frontier...*You* are!" The Vulcan replies, "Indeed. Then perhaps, Jim," he suggests, leaning closer to whisper softly into one ear, "we should...boldly go...where no man has gone before." This erotic exchange is mapped onto the realization that they *must* return to the future so that they can have existed to be able to go back into the past to make sure that *Star Trek* gets produced, the world gets saved, and humans go into space. (Kirk has a hard time following this, but fortunately the more intellectual Spock grasps the intricacies and paradoxes of time travel.) The novel ends with their dramatic rescue by the female security officer of the *Enterprise*.

The popularity of Black's *Dreams of the Sleepers* and its two sequels lies in the way she is able to elaborate her idea of "technomysticism" to express the deepest wish of *Star Trek* fan culture: that the fandom matters, that what the fans do can affect the world in significant ways. However, it is not enough for the critic to identify this wish and be satisfied with designating it as a *symptom* — of the fans' need, for example, for an imaginary family or community, or as a substitute for their lack of real social agency or cultural capital. This is the way fan culture is usually discussed.[78] The conceptual strength of slash writing forces us to see that it is more interesting to look at what the fans are *doing* with this individually and collectively elaborated discourse than it is to discuss what it "represents." And, because this discourse is so imbued with utopian longings ("to free the individual, through leisure, technology, and self-realization, to go out and meet others as equals instead of enemies"[79]), it also begs a reconsideration of the role and value of utopian thinking, especially when this form of popular argument is carried out in and through a mass-culture product, and by the relatively disempowered.

FUTURE MEN

The K/Sers are constantly asking themselves why they are drawn to writing their sexual and social utopian romances across the bodies of two men, and why these two men in particular. Their answers range from the pleasures of writing explicit same-sex erotica to the fact that writing a story about two men avoids the built-in inequality of the romance formula, in which dominance and submission are invariably the respective roles of men and women. There are also advantages to writing about a futuristic couple: it is far from incidental that women have chosen to write their erotic stories about a couple living in a fully automated world in which there will never be fights over who has to scrub the tub, take care of the kids, cook, or do the laundry. Indeed, one reason the fans give for their difficulty in slashing *Star Trek: The Next Generation* is that children and families now live on the *Enterprise* (albeit in a detachable section!), and that those circumstances severely limit the erotic possibilities.

All the same, one still wonders why these futuristic bodies — this couple of the twenty-third century — must be imagined and written as male bodies. Why are the women fans so alienated from their own bodies that they can write erotic fantasies only in relation to a nonfemale body? Some who have thought about this question, fans and critics alike, have tried to show that Kirk and Spock are not coded as male but are rather androgynous, even arguing that this was the case on the original show. Slash readers and writers would then be identifying with and eroticizing characters who combine traits of masculinity and femininity. However, the more I read of the slash literature, the more I am convinced that Kirk and Spock are clearly meant to be male. Understanding this helps to answer the question about the women fans' alienation from their own bodies. For the bodies from which these women are alienated are twentieth-century women's bodies: bodies that are a legal, moral, and religious battleground, that are the site of contraceptive failure, that are seen to pose *the* greatest potential danger to the fetuses they house, that are held to painfully higher standards of physical beauty than those of the other sex. Rejecting the perfect Amazons of female fantasy/sword-and-sorcery writing, the K/Sers opt instead for the project of at least *trying* to write real men. (From what I have seen and read in the fandom, I would argue that it is indeed a rejection of the Amazons' perceived artificiality and not a rejection of lesbianism, even though most of the K/Sers are heterosexual.)

What must be remembered also is the K/Sers' penchant for "making do": when asked why they do not create original characters who could be women as well as men, they most often respond that they are just "working with what's out there." In this case it happens to be the world of television, an arena typically populated with strong male characters with whom to identify and take as erotic objects. The writers also insist that one can enter the *Star Trek* world through the male characters only, since the female characters, like Lt. Uhura, Nurse Chapel, and Yeoman Rand, were so marginalized on the show by the sketchiness of their roles and the feminine stereotyping to which they were subjected.

The desire to write real men can be carried out only within a project of retooling masculinity itself, which is precisely what K/S writing sets out to do. It is for this reason as well that Kirk and Spock must be clearly male and not mushily androgynous. This "retooling" is made easier by locating it in a science fiction universe that is both futuristic and offers several generic tropes that prove useful to the project. Feminists, as well as the fans in their daily lives, have had to confront the fact that we may not see the hoped-for "new" or "transformed" men in our lifetimes, and if the truth be told, we often ridicule the efforts of men who try to remake themselves along feminist lines (as Donna Haraway says, "I'd rather go to bed with a cyborg than a sensitive man").[80] The idea of sexual equality, which will necessarily require a renovated masculinity, is taking a long time to become a lived reality and is hard to imagine, much less write.

This difficulty can be seen, for example, in the unsatisfying attempt to rewrite male romance characters in the Silhouette Desire "Man of the Month" series. Each volume features a male protagonist trying to come to terms with his identity and his sexuality in a world that no longer gives clear messages about what will count as "masculinity" but still threatens dire consequences for those men who fail to attain it. In trying to explore male subjectivity, the series' authors are admirably trying to go beyond the "male semiotics" project that almost all feminist critics of the romance have identified as central to the romance narrative. In that narrative, the heroine must learn to read and recode what seems to be, at the beginning of the novel, a cold or even brutish indifference on the part of the hero, so that by the end she has completed the mental work necessary to understanding the perfectly good reasons for his aggressively bad behavior (for example, he had been misinformed by a rival that she was a tramp, a goldigger, or a manhater). The typical romance novel, then, critics say, serves to adjust the female reader to a patriarchal world where she must do all of the mental work of understanding and even forgiving her oppressor. (At least contemporary romance novels no longer require heroines to recode a rape as a simple "miscommunication.") The problem with the "Man of the Month" series is that the male characters are so feebly and unconvincingly sketched out that it is both painful and distasteful to have to share the man's consciousness. More implausible yet is the heroine's passion, if only because it is so hard to believe that anyone would want these guys!

But Kirk and Spock, as rewritten by the slashers, are another matter. If it has become difficult to imagine new men in the present day, then it may be easier to imagine them in a time yet to come. *Surely*, three hundred years from now things will be better. In the slash stories, Kirk and Spock *are* sensitive, as well as kind, strong, thoughtful, and humorous. But their being "sensitive" carries with it none of the associations of wimpiness or smug self-congratulation that it does in the present day. Only in the future, it seems, will it be possible to conceive that yielding phallic power does not result in psychic castration or a demand to be extravagantly praised for having relinquished that power. But Kirk and

Spock are rarely written as perfect; they too have to do some work on themselves. Although the characters are provided with the SF device of the Vulcan mind link, which allows them to communicate more intimately than today's men are thought to do, Kirk and Spock are typically shown learning to overcome the conditioning that prevents them from expressing their feelings. Spock, whose Vulcan training has led him to suppress his emotions totally, has to learn to accept his human or emotional side, since he is, after all, half human. And Kirk, raised an Iowa farm boy, must first recognize and then reject now-archaic ideas of masculinity that were the product of his extremely conventional upbringing. Many slash stories relegate "action" to the background to ensure the tightest possible focus on the two men undergoing this painful yet liberatory process of self-discovery and learning to communicate their feelings. A Romulan attack—will it destroy the *Enterprise*?!—may be the catalyst and context for a weighted exchange of looks, secret caresses, and anguished, revealing intimacies, which no one else on the bridge is supposed to notice, even though Kirk and Spock might carry on like that for forty pages.

And although it is true that, by the fans' own admission, they usually "heterosexualize" Kirk and Spock's sexual practices,[81] often the major sign that Kirk and Spock are different from today's men is that they can freely discuss their own homosexual tendencies and not be insulted or afraid if someone takes them for a gay couple. There is a perfectly understandable idealization of the gay male couple in this fan writing, because such a couple, after all, is one in which love and work can be shared by two equals (a state of affairs the fans feel to be almost unattainable for a heterosexual couple). But there is also a comprehension of the fact that *all* men (and women) must be able to recognize their own homosexual tendencies if they are to have any hope of fundamentally changing oppressive sexual roles. So, too, the fans appreciate gay men's efforts to redefine masculinity, and feel a sense of solidarity with them insofar as gay men also inhabit bodies that are a legal, moral, and religious battleground.

But slash does not stop with retooling the male psyche; it goes after the body as well. Some changes are cosmetic, others go deeper. Spock, for example, has extra erogenous zones (especially the tips of his pointed ears) and a triple-ridged penis. But the greatest change concerns the plot device of *pon farr*, the heat suffered every seven years by all Vulcan males. The man goes into a blood fever (*plak tow*), can become very violent, and will die if he does not have sex, preferably with a mate. The slash fans are not making this up—in the thirty-fourth episode of *Star Trek* (written by Theodore Sturgeon), Spock goes into *pon farr*, begins to die, and is taken back to Vulcan by his comrades so that he can complete the mating ritual and live. *Pon farr* stories are so popular with the slash fans that a zine called *Fever* has been started to publish only *pon farr* stories. I think the fans relish these stories, in part, because they like the idea of men too being subject to a hormonal cycle, and indeed their version of Spock's pre–*pon farr* and *plak tow* symptoms are wickedly and humorously made to parallel those of PMS and menstruation, in a playful and transgressive leveling of the biological playing field. Another nice touch is that Kirk, because he is empathically bonded with the Vulcan through the mind link, does not have to be told when Spock is getting ready to go into *pon farr* or how he is feeling; in fact, he often shares Spock's symptoms.

But perhaps the most extreme retooling of the male body is seen in the stories in which Kirk and Spock have a baby. Few of these stories exist and they are generally reviewed negatively by the fans, who feel that the premise is too farfetched, even for them, and that, finally, pregnancy and child-rearing responsibilities get in the way of erotic fantasies. In one such story, Kirk and Spock are able to have a baby only after Dr. McCoy does a great deal of genetic engineering to create a fertilized ovum, and Scotty a great deal of mechanical and electronic engineering to build an exterior womb. Not only does it take four men to have a baby in this story (!), but the very awkwardness of the apparatus (at the level of story and discourse) and the fans' rejection of most Kirk-and-Spock-have-a-baby stories suggest that some feats of bodily technology, especially when they involve such substantial regendering, are still unimaginable and unwritable.

In slash fandom and the writing practice that it supports, we find a powerful instance of the strength of the popular wish to think through and debate the issues of women's relation to the technologies of science, the mind, and the body, in both fiction and everyday life. Much can be learned from the way the slashers make individual and collective decisions about how they will use technology at home, at work, and at leisure, and how they creatively reimagine their world through making a tactics of technology itself. Even more can be learned by understanding how these tactics are only the latest performance of this popular wish.

"UNPERCEIVED UTOPIAS"

As strange and even aberrant as the slash fans' activities might seem at first glance, their oddness quickly fades when viewed through the lens of contemporary feminist criticism on nineteenth-century women's communities (both real and imagined) and writing practices. "In life as in literature, scholars are uncovering unperceived utopias," Nina Auerbach says in *Communities of Women*.[82] She goes on to cite Carroll Smith-Rosenberg's influential essay, "The Female World of Love and Ritual," which describes the intensity of shared emotions and attachments between nineteenth-century American women "not as an aberration from a norm or a sublimation of a norm gone wrong, but as a natural growth and source of strength."[83] (Or, as a Christmas card I received from two slash fans put it: "Slash fandom—as close as two straight women can get!") Auerbach's description of the nineteenth-century Anglo-American scene could just as well describe today's slashers:

Women in literature who evade the aegis of men also evade traditional categories of definition. Since a community of women is a furtive, unofficial, often underground entity, it can be defined by the complex, shifting, often contradictory attitudes it evokes. Each community defines itself as a "distinct existence," flourishing outside familiar categories and calling for a plurality of perspectives and judgments.

Auerbach is, however, more concerned with the images of

community in women's literature of some standing, like *Little Women*, *Pride and Prejudice*, or *Villette*, than either female communities that existed in fact rather than fiction or popular writing of little artistic or professional status. Slash writing is clearly more reminiscent of the writing practices of women's popular fiction, whether called "domestic," "sentimental," or "sensational." Eschewing traditional claims to artistry, genius, and literary professionalism, nineteenth-century domestic novelists used stereotyped characters and sensational, formulaic plots to educate, entertain, and move their vast, largely female audiences. Crafting an idiom that blended women's domestic, social, and political concerns with a wish to reorganize culture from the woman's point of view, this "damned mob of scribbling women" (as Nathaniel Hawthorne called them) authorized themselves to write trenchant critiques of American society in the face of scorn and disgust for their popularity and perceived lack of literary quality.

As described by literary historian Nina Baym, the prototypical women's novel was one in which a female protagonist struggled against adversity and, on the basis of her independent ability, found success in her own terms.[84] But because this story of feminine development is set in a social context, the fiction contains implicit, if not always explicit, social commentary:

> Indirectly at least, women were beginning to articulate and take a stand on some social issues in their fiction. Opinions on temperance and slavery are often expressed, but other matters are more basic to the structure of these novels. Besides the running attack on the predominance of market-

place values in every area of American life, woman's fiction took especial cognizance of rural-urban tensions and the class divisions in American society. (45)

Although the slashers are writing for much smaller audiences—in fact, largely for themselves—their work nonetheless embodies the same impulse as the female nineteenth-century popular novelists: to transform the public sphere by imaginatively demonstrating how it could be improved through making it more answerable to women's interests. With the slashers, as we have seen, this reshaping takes the form of folding concerns about inner space into the language of outer space, in a kind of narrative Möbius strip, where home and the frontier are finally on the same continuum. Such a movement has its twentieth-century precedent in what media scholar Lynn Spigel has called the 1960s fantastic family sitcom, "a hybrid genre that mixed the conventions of the suburban sit-com past with the space-age imagery of the New Frontier. Programs like *I Dream of Jeannie, My Favorite Martian, The Jetsons*, and *Lost in Space* were premised on an uncanny mixture of suburbia and space travel."[85] Spigel's description of these shows helps to explain why Captain Kirk's command chair looks like a Barcalounger and the deck of the *Enterprise* like a suburban rumpus room, with everyone playing electronic games, watching large-screen television, and carrying on conversations mediated through talking back to the TV set.

But in thus relocating domestic space in outer space, the slashers have boldly gone where no "ink-stained Amazons" of the nineteenth century have gone before. Although some domestic novel heroines were sent West to take part in a civilizing movement of creating garden cities in the wilderness (thus at once taming the city and the wilderness), the majority of them worked from the home in their effort to overturn "the male money system as the law of American life"(Baym 47). The slashers, by contrast, locate their heroes in "Space: the final frontier...," thus implicitly rejecting the separate-sphere ideology that characterized the domestic novel, an ideology that severely limited the transformation of the public sphere to modeling it after the private sphere of the woman-centered home. And the fact that the slash protagonist is not a heroine but two heroes puts a novel spin on what literary theorist Jane Tompkins calls the "cultural work" of American fiction, the work of expressing and shaping the social context that produces the novels.[86] What is that "cultural work" when a community of women writers that produces a twentieth-century version of domestic fiction sets out collectively to elaborate the frontier or male quest novel, a form of American fiction considered the antithesis (and even the enemy) of the domestic or sentimental novel?

From D.H. Lawrence's discovery of a linked mythos of escape and immaculate male love in America's literary canon to Leslie Fiedler's own discovery that Huck and Jim were "queer as three dollar bills," the Sacred Marriage of males has been identified as key to understanding the psychosocial and political unconscious of American fiction.[87] The male couple in the wilderness or on the high seas, always one light and the other dark — Dana's narrator and the *kanaka*, Hope; Cooper's Natty Bumppo and Chingachgook; Melville's Ishmael and Queequeg; Twain's

Huck and Jim—represent for both Lawrence and Fiedler the absolute wilderness in which the stuffiness of home yields to the wigwam, and "my wife" to the natural primitivism of the colored man. In this Eden, the new Adam, the boy who will not grow up, lives in innocent antimarriage with a Noble Red Man. Fiedler first demonstrated this American *mythos*, and its deeply nostalgic appeal, in his famous 1948 essay "Come Back to the Raft Ag'in, Huck Honey!" In 1982 he returned to this topic to question the essay's optimism and to insist on the centrality and persistence of the myth of interethnic male bonding: "The Jew Starsky and the Gentile Hutch, the black Tenspeed and the white Brownshoe, the earthling Captain Kirk and the Vulcan Mr. Spock...[are the] descendants of Natty Bumppo and Chingachgook" (157). He delights in the wide popular reception of his prescient queering of American literature by noting that an early newspaper review of *Star Trek* was headlined, "COME BACK TO THE SPACESHIP AG'IN, SPOCK HONEY."

Why, Fiedler asks, should the Negro and the homosexual become stock literary themes in American fiction and why should these themes have become so bound up with each other? The mythos of interethnic male bonding, he says, both reveals and conceals two essential aspects of American life: the homosocial bonds that structure U.S. culture and the bitter fact of racism. Interethnic male bonding is a fantasy of immaculate passion with no possibility of miscegenation (the men do not really have sex, even though the stories are wildly homoerotic) and astonishing reconciliation, with the white man folded in the arms of his dark beloved and forgiven everything: "'Honey' or 'Aikane'; he will comfort us, as if our offense against him were long ago remitted, were never truly *real*" (Fiedler 150). The reconciliation is an astonishing one because it requires that someone victimized in the extreme does the forgiving. Dana's Hope is dying of the white man's syphilis; Queequeg is racked by fever; Cooper's Indian is aged and hopelessly depressed over the dying of his race; Jim is loaded down with chains, and so on. Similarly, the slashers typically depict Spock as periodically ravaged by *pon farr*, achingly lonely because he is neither human nor Vulcan but something in between, and secretly humiliated by those who mock his devil-like appearance. And in the second *Star Trek* movie, he dies a painful death by radiation, his skin falling from his flesh, sacrificing himself to save others. Fiedler also notes that "the immense gulf of guilt must not be mitigated any more than the disparity of color. Queequeg is not merely brown but monstrously tattooed; Chingachgook is horrid with paint, Jim is portrayed as 'the sick A-rab died blue.'" Spock, of course, is green. And indeed one of the most recurrent and affecting scenes in slash fiction is Spock cradling Jim and calling him "Thy'la," Vulcan for bondmate.

But what is Spock's race? Many *Star Trek* fan writers, not just the slashers, delight in writing stories about Vulcan culture and history. Since this is science fiction, Kirk and Spock can use both warp drive and time travel to get them handily to the planet Vulcan and into an exploration of its past. The history and prehistory of Vulcan is almost invariably written by the fans as an exoticized Asian martial arts culture or a romanticized Native American culture. Never, except for rare efforts to Egyptianize Vulcan history, do the fans touch on anything even remotely

African. Although Fiedler thinks a man of any color will do to stand in for the fantasy of the Negro, it is significant that the slash fans consistently avoid writing Vulcan culture and history—and Spock's race—as African or African American. They prefer to orientalize or romanticize the color divide in a strategic yet unconscious evasion of what has historically in the U.S. been the most bitterly contentious racial division.

"Home as Heaven, Home as Hell" is the title Fiedler gave to the 1982 essay in which he takes back the optimism of "Come Back to the Raft Ag'in, Huck Honey." In this essay he reconsiders his earlier relegation of the domestic and sentimental novels to "subliterature" lacking in "tragic ambivalence or radical protest" and his corresponding belief that the "masculine" sentimentality of a male writer like Cooper was superior to the "feminine" pathos of a female writer like Stowe. Fiedler says he now realizes that it is not just "the dream of racial reconciliation" that determines that the antiwife must be nonwhite but also the "nightmare of misogyny" that says the antiwife must be nonfemale. It is a misogyny, he says, in a peculiarly American form, a view of women which identifies them with everything that must be escaped in order to be free.

There are thus two myths here, working dialectically, which allows this symbolic resolution:

The myth of the wilderness companions represents also the male ex-European's dream of effecting—behind the backs of white women, as it were—a reconciliation with those fellow males we know we have really, *really*, oppressed. (153)

TREK

The reconciliation, Fiedler emphasizes, must be a marriage of the spirit, never the flesh. "Our anti-heroes," he says, "do not flee white women to beget red/brown/black/yellow children neither white nor nonwhite." Is it the horror of miscegenation haunting these texts that also rears its ugly head in the slash fans' resistance to the technologically miraculous Kirk-and-Spock-have-a-baby stories? Probably not, because the miscegenation has already happened: Spock is the offspring of a human mother, Amanda, and a Vulcan father, Sarek, who are lovingly written by the fans as one of the few positive heterosexual couples to appear in slash fiction.

While the slash fans are undoubtedly complicit with a traditional American tendency to obscure racism and racial tensions (both in their writing and the everyday life of the fandom), they are also engaged in collectively elaborating a story that goes a long way toward untangling and recasting this double American mythos of misogyny and racial reconciliation.[88] In this respect, it is significant that the slashers celebrate the miscegenation that resulted in the birth of Spock and depict Kirk and Spock's marriage as very much of the flesh, not only allowing but extolling a male-male relation that is overtly homoerotic. Fiedler argues that overt homosexuality threatens to compromise "an essential aspect of American sentimental life: the comraderie of the locker room and ball park, the good fellowship of the poker game and fishing trip, a kind of passionless passion...possessing an innocence above suspicion" (143). Christopher Newfield, writing in the wake of the emergence of queer studies and Eve Kosofsky Sedgwick's idea of "homosexual panic," takes even further than

139

Fiedler the specification of what it is in American culture that is threatened by overt homosexuality.[89] Homophobia, Newfield says, is politically charged by a phobia about equality:

> Male homoeroticism, when it becomes public homosexuality, threatens not just male but *military* order. It threatens the widely fetishized "unit cohesion" rooted in the despotism of unchallenged leaders. It threatens to undermine the despotism that has symbolically and in fact stabilized democratic society; it threatens by challenging not just straight homosociality in general, but a male homosociality that consists of submission to superiors. (30)

In a broad tradition most famously articulated in the U.S. by Walt Whitman, Newfield says, "homoeroticism figures a faith in radical democracy." This tradition is one of a "brotherly love" that fuses sexual and political identity to defeat the competitive hierarchy "that mainstream U.S. culture works especially hard to cast as the only viable mode of personal freedom" (30).

When the history of slash fandom is written (not by me, but others, likely the fans themselves), it will also have to be a history of the extreme hostility that many "regular" *Star Trek* fans have shown toward the slashers. The Trekkers have had to struggle mightily, however, to find the right language to deride and dismiss the slashers. After all, Trekdom is a culture that believes itself superior to the rest of U.S. society in the strength of its allegiance to the values of democratic equality and tolerance for differences. Trekkers are therefore reluctant to criticize the slashers in overtly sexist or homophobic language, usually falling back on "We wouldn't want children at conventions to accidentally be exposed to this stuff" or "It's an insult to Gene Roddenberry's vision." But Trekkers are also people devoted to reimagining the world through a stubbornly militaristic fiction, barely disguised as Yankee adventurism even in *Next Generation*'s more corporate-bureaucratic version of it. (Captain Picard usually takes an anguished meeting with his senior officers before bagging the Prime Directive.) The slash version of *Star Trek* threatens the Trekkers because it is not only sexually but politically scary, with its overt homoeroticism throwing into sharp relief the usually invisible homosocial underpinnings of Trekdom, the Federation, and U.S. culture.

How do the slashers deal with the other side of all this, Fiedler's "nightmare of misogyny"? As Sedgwick has shown, misogyny lies not only in the exclusion of women but in requiring them to legitimize the bonds between men with their real or symbolic presence. The ethics of how to treat women characters is, in fact, one of the most discussed topics in slash fandom. "Mary Sue" stories, as the fans call them, are utterly reviled, even though such stories are often the first story that a fan will write. A "Mary Sue" is any story where a young, bright, gorgeous new ensign (usually a transparent stand-in for the author) falls head over heels for Kirk or Spock. This is too close to the "sentimental love religion" of the romance novel for the slashers to stomach. The fans also reject stories in which a woman serves as a mere bridge or relay between the two men.

In one much criticized story, Lt. Uhura realizes the unarticulated passion that Kirk and Spock feel for each other but knows that neither one, especially the repressed Spock, will ever make a move. She seduces Spock to blow the lid off all that passion and then tenderly talks to him until he finally understands the true direction of his desire. After Kirk and Spock are united, she graciously steps aside. It is no wonder that fans vociferously rejected this scenario because slash ethics determine that the women characters in the *Star Trek* fictional universe, minor though they may be, are to be written about respectfully and never used just to get the two men together, to either enable or legitimize that relation. Slash fiction, then, is careful to avoid the misogyny Fiedler rightly found to be the necessary complement to the symbolic resolution of "the bad dream of genocide." Even though women have been largely written out of slash fiction, women's interests have not. As we shall see, writing the women out of this traditional scenario is the surest way for those interests to get expressed.

Literary theorist Joseph Allen Boone argues that the quest romance as written by men has not invariably valorized ideological concerns that our culture has designated "masculine" or "patriarchal."[90] He agrees with Fiedler that the male quest romance was an unconscious rebellion against the ethos of sexual polarity pervading sentimental treatments of love and seduction throughout the history of the novel. It was, Boone argues, meant to be an alternative to the antagonistic sexual relationships emanating from the novel's "sentimental love religion." But he also insists that leaving the constraints of traditionally defined manhood does not have to be escapist or regressive: "The outward voyage to confront the unknown that by definition constitutes quest narrative simultaneously traces an inner journey toward a redefinition, a 'remaking' of self that defies, at least partially, social convention and sexual categorization" (228-229).

And indeed, Boone finds in the very novels that Fiedler discusses visions of selfhood and mutual relationship that attempt to "break down conventional sexual categorization by breaking through the limiting forms of culture and the conventions of love literature at once." Such a rejection of institutional marriage can have several important advantages. Where there is mutuality of gender there is, at least in theory, a degree of equal interchange and individuality that is often automatically negated in the conventional marital union:

> As a result, these questing comrades often evolve multifaceted relationships that daringly blur the boundaries separating literary subject and object: their loving bonds simultaneously partake of brotherly, passionate, paternal, filial, even maternal qualities, without being restricted to one role or model alone. (236)

Nothing better exemplifies the way slash writers have developed precisely such a model of equality and individuality, while exploring every permutation of Kirk's and Spock's roles, than the 1991 publication *The 25th Year*, described on the cover page as "a collaborative K/S novel celebrating twenty-five years of *Star Trek*...and the infinite diversity of the love of Kirk and Spock." Edited by Alexis Fegan Black and issued by Pon Farr Press, *The 25th Year* brings together over thirty writers, poets, and artists to write the story of Kirk and Spock from their first meeting to growing old together. In an editorial, Black writes of the "magic" of pulling this anthology together, as authors and artists working separately wrote amazingly complementary stories, taking up and expanding on ideas and plot points already anticipated by the other writers. She goes on to tell how she wrote a frame story for all the contributions and a few linking stories to fill in the gaps.

The major dramatic thread of the stories (passing through Klingon battles, Romulan treachery, Vulcan machinations, Federation bureaucracy, and much more) is Kirk trying to convince Spock that he, Kirk, is really a bottom and wants their sex to be rougher, much rougher, even than the violent madness of *pon farr*. After all, he has to be captain all day, always responsible and in charge; at night and in bed he wants someone else to give the orders. Enough of Spock folding him into his arms, tenderly making love to him, comforting him, nurturing him, calling him "Thy'la," he wants to be fucked and fucked hard. Not every time, just often enough to restore a mutuality of emotion that alone makes the bond between them come alive. Spock resists, because hard sex and the fierce emotions that come with it remind him of the violent passions that so roiled Vulcan culture before a collective decision was made to construct a society based on the suppression of all emotion. So, too (how nineties!), his fear of hard sex is given an elaborate psychological basis in infantile sexual trauma: as a child he accidentally overheard his parents having sex during his father's *pon farr* and mistook the screams and groans of his mother as cries of fear and pain. Jim asks him to consider that perhaps they were the sounds of pleasure. Spock finally comes around, assuring the mutuality of their relation, now at every level. The front and back covers of *The 25th Year*, reproduced here, artistically document the movement toward that final resolution.

To make slash fiction do the "cultural work" the fans want it to do, the slashers have ingeniously rewritten and recast the American mythos of interethnic male bonding by making that relationship homoerotic rather than homosocial. Ensuring the democratic equality of the pair, the slashers have eliminated its racism by celebrating miscegenation and avoided the misogyny inherent in the mythos by respecting the women characters and never using them to further the male-male bond. It is thus not only fascinating (as Spock would say) but logical (as Spock would also say) that amateur women writers around the country would, in the early 1970s, "spontaneously" get the idea of writing their sexual and social utopias through a futuristic and technologized version of the Sacred Marriage of males.

POPULAR SEX

The slash scenario does not follow the typical route of feminist utopian fiction. Contemporary "feminist fabulations" such as Joanna Russ's *The Female Man* and Marge Piercy's *Woman on the Edge of Time* descend from the work of nineteenth-century women writers of scientific-social utopias who created original fictional universes peopled by women only, or women vastly superior to the male inhabitants of those utopias. The most notable include Charlotte Perkins Gilman's *Herland* (1915), Alice Ilgenfritz Jones and Ella Merchant's *Unveiling a Parallel: A Romance* (1893), and Mary Bradley Lane's *Mizora: A Prophecy* (1881). The slashers, however, think and write in a "found" universe, the already given fictional world of *Star Trek* and, by extension, the cultural narrative that is NASA/TREK.

When the slashers are asked "Why *Star Trek*? Why television?," they respond by saying, "We write in relation to what's out there, and what's out there is television." At a 1996 slash convention one fan who was moderating a panel on "Perceptions of Slash" asked a room full of fans whether they were more embarrassed to be known as pornographers or TV lovers by friends, family, and co-workers. Overwhelmingly, they said (to rueful laughter) that it was much worse to be thought of as an avid consumer of television than as a producer of sexually explicit work. "Pornographer," at least, has some cachet, especially for a woman, but "TV fan" has only pejorative connotations, especially for a woman. The boldness, then, of the slashers' version of "boldly going where no one has gone before," is not so much their move into a hitherto male practice of illicit sexual representation but their intervention in the vast space of television industry mass production. Their rewriting of the TREK side of the NASA/TREK story relies in very large part, however, on the shock of the taboo sex they introduce into it, in the tradition that dates from the sixteenth-century of using pornography as a populist, often revolutionary, vehicle to attack and transform hegemonic ideas and powerful institutions.[91]

The slash version of *Star Trek*—an underground fiction produced by women that is illicitly sexual, homoerotic, egalitarian, and antiracist—offers the sharpest possible challenge to the NASA side of the NASA/TREK story. Slash writing devotes as much time to inner space as to outer space, emphasizes women's inclusion and creative control, and offers a much more satisfying utopian solution than NASA has yet been able to conceive. But a slashed NASA/TREK is popular science at its best. It is an experiment in imagining new forms of sexual and racial equality, democracy, and a fully human relation to the world of science and technology. NASA/TREK is a much needed utopian narrative of and for our time.

NOTES

[1]Carl Sagan, *The Demon-Haunted World: Science as a Candle in the Dark* (New York: Random House, 1995). Sagan died just as my book was going to press. I have left my criticisms of his approach as I originally stated them because his work will surely continue to influence what we think about science and popular culture for a long time to come. In a piece written shortly before Sagan's death that appeared just after it, biologist Richard Lewontin makes a similar criticism of Sagan's hectoring antipopulism. "Billions and Billions of Demons," *New York Review of Books* (January 9, 1997): 28-32.

[2]For some of the best descriptions of people who think science is too important to be left to the scientists, see David J. Hess, *Science in the New Age: The Paranormal, Its Defenders and Debunkers, and American Culture* (Madison: University of Wisconsin Press, 1993), and Andrew Ross, "New Age Technoculture," in *Cultural Studies*, ed. Lawrence Grossberg, Cary Nelson, and Paula Treichler (New York: Routledge, 1992).

[3]Reported in *Science* 269 (August 4, 1995).

[4]A forthcoming book, *Enterprise Zones: Liminal Positions on* Star Trek, ed. Kent Ono, Elyce Rae Helford, Sarah Projansky, and Taylor Harrison, aims to offer the first comprehensive overview of the emblematic cultural status of *Star Trek* fiction and fandom, with an annotated bibliography of critical work on *Star Trek*.

[5]Whoopi Goldberg, too, had been so moved as a child by seeing an African-American woman on the deck of the *Enterprise* that she begged Gene Roddenberry for a role on *Star Trek: The Next Generation* so that she in turn could show young African Americans that they could go into space. Roddenberry gladly gave Goldberg the role of the infinitely old and wise Guinan, the alien bartender-confidante of the Ten Forward Lounge. Nichols, Jemison, and Goldberg all make appearances at *Star Trek* conventions, sometimes together.

[6]"Another Final Frontier: *Star Trek* at a Museum," *New York Times*, March 3, 1995. Mary Henderson was the curator of *Star Trek: The Exhibition*.

[7]These are the jokes I heard. Patrick D. Morrow attempted to collect all the jokes in "Those Sick Challenger Jokes," *Journal of Popular Culture* 20, no. 4 (Spring 1987): 175-184. Here are some of the sick jokes he found that echo the ones I heard:

> *Do you know what Christa McAuliffe's last words were to her husband?*
> "You feed the dog and I'll feed the fish."
> *How do we know that Christa McAuliffe didn't have dandruff?*
> They found her head and shoulders on the beach.
> *Do you know what color Christa McAuliffe's eyes were?*
> They were blue. One blew over this way and one blew over that way.

Jokelorist Alan Dundes says, "The available evidence strongly suggests that sick joke cycles constitute a kind of collective mental hygienic defense mechanism that allows people to cope with the most dire of disasters, natural or otherwise. Deploring the resultant jokes serves little purpose. They would not come into existence if they did not answer some sort of deep psychological need." This formulation is taken from one of many essays Dundes has written on sick jokes and other forms of "low" humor, "At Ease, Disease—AIDS Jokes as Sick Humor," *American Behavioral Scientist*, no. 1 (January/February 1987): 72-81.

[8]For one of the best, historically informed discussions of the ways

male fears of women and technology have been conflated, see Andreas Huyssen's chapter, "The Vamp in the Machine: Fritz Lang's *Metropolis*," in *After the Great Divide: Modernism, Mass Culture, Postmodernism* (Bloomington: Indiana University Press, 1986). Another excellent discussion, which focuses specifically on the American Cold War imaginary, is Elaine Tyler May's "Explosive Issues: Sex, Women, and the Bomb," in *Recasting America: Culture and Politics in the Age of the Cold War* (Chicago: University of Chicago Press, 1989).

[9]Robert T. Hohler was the *Concord* (N.H.) *Monitor* reporter assigned to cover Christa McAuliffe from the moment of her selection. His biography of her, *I Touch the Future*, is full of valuable information about the ways NASA and the media promoted the Teacher in Space program and characterized McAuliffe as the ordinary citizen in space. Although Hohler felt the need to shape McAuliffe's story as one of sacrifice and inspiration, much of what Hohler reported can be read very differently, as I have done here.

[10]Thanks to Joel Pfister for pointing this out to me. His description of the social imaginary of nineteenth-century American women factory workers can be found in *The Production of Personal Life: Class, Gender, and the Psychological in Hawthorne's Fiction* (Stanford: Stanford University Press, 1991), esp. p. 118. See also Mary P. Ryan, "Femininity and Capitalism in Antebellum America," in *Capitalist Patriarchy and the Case for Socialist Feminism*, ed. Zillah Eisenstein (New York: Monthly Review Press, 1977).

[11]Joseph J. Trento, *Prescription for Disaster: From the Glory of Apollo to the Betrayal of the Shuttle* (New York: Crown Publishers, 1987), p. 250.

[12]*Challenger* (ABC, 1989) was directed by George Englund. The best part of this film is the casting: Christa McAuliffe is played by Karen Allen, who was the spunky heroine of *Raiders of the Lost Ark*; Captain Mike Smith is played by Bruce Kerwin, now a gay icon for his roles in *Longtime Companion* and *Torchsong Trilogy*; and mission specialist Dr. Ronald E. McNair is played by Joe Morton, who was both the Brother from Another Planet and the man responsible for 3 billion

deaths in *Terminator 2*.

[13]These jokes are from Elizabeth Radin Simons, "The NASA Joke Cycle: The Astronauts and the Teacher," *Western Folklore* 44, no. 4 (October 1986): 243-260.

[14]Morrow, "Those Sick Challenger Jokes."

[15]Patricia Mellencamp, "TV Time and Catastrophe, or *Beyond the Pleasure Principle* of Television," in *Logics of Television: Essays in Cultural Criticism*, ed. Patricia Mellencamp (Bloomington: Indiana University Press, 1990).

[16]Dale Carter, *The Final Frontier* (London: Verso, 1988). For an in-depth study of NASA's decline from an ambitious R & D project to one dominated by commercial and military interests, see Trento, *Prescription for Disaster*.

[17]Richard Feynman was a physicist who served on the Presidential Commission on the Space Shuttle *Challenger* Accident. In *"What Do You Care What Other People Think?"* (New York: W.W. Norton, 1988), a collection of anecdotes about his life in science, Feynman discusses his experiences on the commission. After interviewing technicians and managers at both the Kennedy and Houston Space Centers, Feynman concluded that the Reagan White House had put no direct pressure on NASA to have the voyage coincide with the State of the Union address. He emphasizes, however, that no pressure was necessary: "I learned, by seeing how they worked, that the people in a big system like NASA *know* what has to be done—*without* being told" (217). In the same way, Feynman's critical remarks about NASA were relegated to an appendix to the commission's report.

[18]Kitty Kelley quotes astrologer Ed Helin on his duties for the Reagan White House: "As President, he was primarily concerned with the timing of events and how his popularity would be affected by his actions. He called me to determine the best timing for invading Grenada, for bombing Libya, for launching the *Challenger*, things like that....I was paid in cash by a local representative of the Republican National Committee....He would come to my house with an envelope of cash

every month or so....No, I can't give you the man's name because I'm still doing astrological work for the Republican National Committee." Kitty Kelley, *Nancy Reagan: The Unauthorized Biography* (New York: Simon and Schuster, 1991), p. 614.

[19]These were the findings of Dr. Joseph P. Kerwin, director of Life Sciences at the Johnson Space Center, who was asked to report on the cause of death of the crew to the Presidential Commission on the Space Shuttle *Challenger* Accident. (*Report to the President* is a government document published in Washington, D.C., June 6, 1986.) A useful discussion of the report can be found in Richard S. Lewis, *Challenger: The Final Voyage* (New York: Columbia University Press, 1988).

[20]Without explanation, NASA released forty-five photographs of the recovered *Challenger* crew cabin debris on February 14, 1993, to New York artist Ben Sarao, who turned them over to the *New York Times*. Sarao got the photographs as the result of an inexplicably successful FOIA lawsuit.

[21]Catharine A. MacKinnon, *Feminism Unmodified: Discourses on Life and Law* (Cambridge, Mass.: Harvard University Press, 1987), p. 223.

[22]Folklorist Jan Harold Brunvand is the main collector of urban legends. His books include *The Vanishing Hitchhiker*, *The Choking Doberman*, *The Mexican Pet*, and *Curses! Broiled Again!* He shows that many such legends concern accidents involving technological failure.

[23]Thanks to Valerie Hartouni for alerting me to the Internet "transcript" of the *Challenger* astronauts' last words.

[24]Michael Taussig gave a paper on the public secret at the University of California, Santa Barbara, on February 24, 1992. He has a short discussion of the logic of the public secret in *Mimesis and Alterity: A Particular History of the Senses* (New York: Routledge, 1993).

[25]Calvin Burch's remarks were reported by Associated Press aerospace writer Marcia Dunn on January 26, 1992, on the sixth anniversary of the *Challenger* disaster.

[26]The Times Wire Services of March 15, 1992, reported the discov-

ery by TIGHAR, The International Group for Historic Aircraft Recovery, which "employed the same technology to find pieces of the space shuttle *Challenger* in the Atlantic."

[27] "Costly Adventuring," *The Outlook* 146, no. 18 (August 31, 1927): 556.

[28] Muriel Earhart Morrissey and Carol L. Osborne, *Amelia, My Courageous Sister: Biography of Amelia Earhart, True Facts About Her Disappearance* (Santa Clara, Calif.: Osborne Publisher, 1987), pp. 76-78.

[29] A few examples of the research on children's responses to viewing the televised disaster are: John C. Wright, Dale Kunkel, Marites Pinon, and Aletha C. Huston, "How Children Reacted to Televised Coverage of the Space Shuttle Disaster," *Journal of Communication* 39, no. 2 (Spring 1989); Delorys Blume et al., "Challenger 10 and Our Schoolchildren: Reflections on the Catastrophe," *Death Studies* 10 (1986); and Lenore Terr, "Close Encounters of the Traumatic Kind," in *Too Scared to Cry: Psychic Trauma and Childhood* (New York: Basic Books, 1990). There are also a number of studies of adult responses to the televised catastrophe.

[30] Terr, *Too Scared to Cry*, p. 329.

[31] Patricia Mellencamp makes good use of Walter Benjamin on Freud and "shock" to give a different answer as to why we have such a strong positional sense in relation to public trauma. She quotes Benjamin: "Perhaps the special achievement of shock defense may be seen in its function of assigning to an incident a precise point in time in consciousness at the cost of the integrity of its contents." She concludes, "The assigning of a time at the cost of content for Benjamin 'would be a peak achievement of the intellect; it would turn the incident into a moment that has been lived'" (253-254). Mellencamp's discussion of the *Challenger* disaster, like Mary Ann Doane's ("Information, Crisis, Catastrophe") is concerned specifically with the role of television in representing and managing our relation to public trauma. Both Doane's essay and Mellencamp's appear in *Logics of Television: Essays in Cultural Criticism*, ed. Patricia Mellencamp (Bloomington: Indiana University Press, 1990).

[32] Neisser's and Harsch's findings were reported in the *Chronicle of*

Higher Education (February 28, 1990).

[33]Sigmund Freud, "Remembering, Repeating and Working-Through (Further Recommendations on the Technique of Psycho-analysis II)" (1914), in *The Standard Edition of the Complete Psychological Works of Sigmund Freud*, ed. James Strachey, vol. 12 (London: Hogarth Press, 1962).

[34]James Gunn, "A Short History of the Space Program; or, A Funny Thing Happened on the Way to the Moon," *Vertrex* 2, no. 1 (April 1974). His comment on the *Challenger* explosion's contribution to reviving the adventure of space travel was made in conversation at the University of Kansas, July 1992.

[35]Michel Serres, *Statues: Le second livre des fondations* (Paris: Editions F. Bourin, 1987), pp. 223-224.

[36]Ibid., p. 223 (my translation).

[37]Paul Virilio, *The Museum of Accidents* (Toronto: Public Access Collective, 1989).

[38]Susan Sontag, "The Imagination of Disaster," in *Film Theory and Criticism*, ed. Gerald Mast and Marshall Cohen (New York: Oxford University Press, 1979).

[39]The *Globe and Mail* published the photograph under the headline "NASA's View of Canada" (February 12, 1992), p. A3. The Canadian Space Agency now disavows the photograph entirely, saying it was Bondar's decision to dress up like a Mountie. A CSA representative told me that this photograph was not an official NASA photograph but a private one made by the crew of the *Discovery* for the eyes of family and friends only, but which was inadvertently released to the newspapers. The representative explained that such a photo shoot is a ritual before every flight and the astronauts get to choose the theme. This time the crew decided to dress up in something very dear to them and Bondar, in her love of Canada and willingness to promote it, chose to dress up as a Mountie. I'm not sure which story is worse: that NASA made Bondar do it or that NASA chose someone who could be counted on to enact this kind of patriotic fervor and contribute to the space agency's "managed diversity."

[40]Roberta Bondar, interview on *Canada AM*, CTV, February 18, 1992.

[41]Kellie Hudson, "Hometown Gets Boost from 'Bondar-mania,'" *Toronto Star* (January 30, 1992).

[42]Linda Richardson, "Sault, Canada Taking Pride as Bondar Shows Right Stuff," *Sault Star* (February 20, 1992), p. C15.

[43]Jack Lakey, "'Not in this program to die': Astronaut Starts Countdown," *Toronto Star* (January 12, 1992), p. D5.

[44]John Colapinto, "High Flying Roberta Bondar," *Chatelaine* (January 1993): 64.

[45]Lakey, *Toronto Star*, p. D5.

[46]In conversation with Robin Moore, who reported it to me.

[47]William J. Broad, "Recipe for Love: A Boy, a Girl, a Spacecraft," *New York Times* (February 11, 1992), p. C1.

[48]Statement made by an unnamed official at Johnson Space Center in Houston, *Washington Post* (May 27, 1987), p. A5.

[49]Ellen Willis, "Now Voyager," in *No More Nice Girls: Countercultural Essays* (Hanover, N.H.: Wesleyan University Press, 1992), pp. 240-243.

[50]Eric Santner made this comment as a respondent to the panel on "Mourning and Melancholia in the Post-Holocaust: Film, History, Psychoanalysis," organized by Dominick LaCapra at the Modern Language Association Convention, December 29, 1992.

[51]"Navy Highly Rated Female Pilot Who Crashed," *New York Times* (AP) (November 21, 1994).

[52]Eric Schmitt, "Pilot's Death Renews Debate Over Women in Combat Role," *New York Times* (November 30, 1994).

[53]Trento, *Prescription for Disaster*.

[54]Diane Vaughan, *The Challenger Launch Decision: Risky Technology, Culture, and Deviance at NASA* (Chicago: University of Chicago Press, 1996). Claus Jensen weaves a good story about the events and behaviors surrounding the *Challenger* disaster in *A Dramatic Narrative about the Challenger Accident and Our Time*, trans. Barbara Haveland (New York: Farrar, Strauss, Giroux, 1996).

[55]Eric J. Chaisson, *The Hubble Wars: Astrophysics Meets Astropolitics in the Two-Billion-Dollar Struggle over the Hubble Space Telescope* (New York: HarperCollins, 1994).

[56]Grace George Corrigan, *A Journal for Christa* (Lincoln and London: University of Nebraska Press, 1993).

[57]Sally Ride, with Susan Okie, *To Space and Back* (New York: Lothrap, Lee, and Shepard Books, 1986).

[58]Helen Sharman and Christopher Priest, *Seize the Moment: The Autobiography of Britain's First Astronaut*, with a foreword by Arthur C. Clarke (London: Victor Gollancz, 1993).

[59]Patricia Limerick, "Imagined Frontiers: Westward Expansion and the Future of the Space Program," in *Space Policy Alternatives*, ed. Radford Byerly, Jr. (Boulder: Westview Press, 1992), pp. 249-261.

[60]Veronica Webb, "No Place Like Home" (interview with Mae Jemison), *Interview* (July 1993): 75-76.

[61]Andrew Lawler, "Goldin Puts NASA on New Trajectory," *Science* 272 (May 10, 1996): 800.

[62]Robert L. Park, "NASA: Goldin Delights Scientists with Speech at AAAS Meeting," in *What's New* (Friday, February 16, 1996) [whatsnew@aps.org].

[63]Dorothy Nelkin, *Selling Science: How the Press Covers Science and Technology*, rev. ed. (New York: W. H. Freeman and Co., 1995).

[64]Stephen Jay Gould's words of praise for NASA in "Life on Mars? So What?," *New York Times* (August 11, 1996), p.A17.

[65]See the "Intimacy in Space" section of Yvonne Clearwater's "A Human Place in Outer Space," *Psychology Today* (July 1985): 43.

[66]My characterizations of *Star Trek* fans are drawn from years of attending conventions, both official and unofficial; reading hundreds of fan publications, again both official and unofficial; and subscribing to a number of newsletters. Of course, there is now an explosion of on-line information and exchange on *Star Trek* and its fandom, which I am barely able to keep up with. Of the newsletters, by far the most interesting

and helpful for understanding regular (as opposed to more underground fandom) is the Connecticut-based *CCSTSG Enterprises*, which describes itself as "a compendium of news and views, with loving and irreverent looks at the *Star Trek* phenomenon and its faithful following." *CCSTSG Enterprises* is available at 7 Quarry Street, Ellington, CT 06029-4147. A check for $9.00 will get you six issues; make check out to "Jeff Mills."

[67]William Shatner, quoted in Allan Asherman, *The Star Trek Interview Book* (New York: Pocket Books, 1988), p. 19.

[68]The producers and writers of *Star Trek*, as well as the principal actors, know about the fan fiction writing that depicts Kirk and Spock as lovers, and several have responded when pressed for their opinions of the fictional pairing (although none admits to having read any of the fan fiction). In his novelization of *Star Trek: The Motion Picture* (New York: Pocket Books, 1979), Gene Roddenberry, the head producer of *Star Trek* and its original creator, adds an editor's note to "report" Kirk's opinion (and, indirectly, Spock's) on the matter. Here, Kirk is purportedly replying to the author's request for clarification:

> I was never aware of this *lovers* rumor, although I have been told that Spock encountered it several times. Apparently he had always dismissed it with his characteristic lifting of his right eyebrow which usually connoted some combination of surprise, disbelief, and/or annoyance. As for myself, although I have no moral or other objections to physical love in any of its many Earthly, alien, and mixed forms, I have always found my best gratification in that creature *woman*. Also, I would dislike being thought of as so foolish that I would select a love partner who came into sexual heat only once every seven years.

David Gerrold, science fiction and *Star Trek* writer who wrote *The World of Star Trek* (New York: Bluejay Books, 1984), takes a much harsher approach to trying to curtail fan desire to rewrite Kirk and

Spock as lovers. He says he realized he could not write a book about *Star Trek* and the fan culture surrounding it without mentioning what he calls "the K/S ladies" (197). He also feels he must say something because even being told by Gene Roddenberry himself that Kirk and Spock are "just friends" has not stopped the K/S fans from projecting their own sexual fantasies onto *Star Trek*, which Gerrold insists is a nuisance to the producers and fans. He claims that "more than one young would-be fan" has been prohibited from attending *Star Trek* conventions or reading the institutionally approved *Star Trek* magazines because his or her parents have seen this material. Pitting women against each other, he quotes one woman fan who objects to the fact that "too many" of the stories involve Kirk and Spock in sadomasochistic scenarios, which, she feels, do not reflect appropriate behavior for two of Star Fleet's finest officers. To round off his attack, Gerrold quotes a gay male *Star Trek* fan who is offended by the depiction of gay men in the K/S writing. Finally, speaking for himself, Gerrold accuses the K/S fans of lacking good manners because they have not followed the rules of Gene Roddenberry's "universe" (121-122).

Fans report that Leonard Nimoy, who plays Spock, has given the best response. Once, at a *Star Trek* convention, he replied to a request to give his opinion of the likelihood of Kirk and Spock being lovers by saying, "I don't know, I wasn't there."

[69] Joanna Russ, "Pornography for Women, by Women, with Love," in *Magic Mommas, Trembling Sisters, Puritans, and Perverts: Feminist Essays* (Trumansburg, N.Y.: Crossing Press, 1985).

[70] See my "Time Travel, Primal Scene, and the Critical Dystopia," in *The Future of an Illusion: Film, Feminism, and Psychoanalysis* (Minneapolis: University of Minnesota Press, 1989).

[71] Sarah Lefanu, *Feminism and Science Fiction* (Bloomington: Indiana University Press, 1989), p. 2. Lefanu mentions the K/S fans, but only very briefly.

[72] Michel de Certeau, *The Practice of Everyday Life*, trans. Steven

Rendall (Berkeley: University of California Press, 1984), p. xx.

⁷³Ibid.

⁷⁴In addition to Joanna Russ's essay, some of the key texts on slash writing are: Patricia Frazer Lamb and Diana L. Veith, "Romantic Myth, Transcendence, and *Star Trek* Zines," in *Erotic Universe: Sexuality and Fantastic Literature* (New York: Greenwood Press, 1986); Henry Jenkins, *Textual Poachers: Television Fans and Participatory Culture* (New York: Routledge, 1992), chap. 6; Camille Bacon-Smith, *Enterprising Women: Television Fandom and the Creation of Popular Myth* (Philadelphia: University of Pennsylvania Press, 1992), chap. 9; Constance Penley, "Feminism, Psychoanalysis, and the Study of Popular Culture," in *Cultural Studies*, ed. Lawrence Grossberg, Cary Nelson, and Paula Treichler (New York: Routledge, 1992) and "Brownian Motion: Women, Tactics, and Technology," in *Technoculture*, ed. Constance Penley and Andrew Ross (Minneapolis: University of Minnesota Press, 1991).

⁷⁵De Certeau, *The Practice of Everyday Life*, p. 18. See Henry Jenkins's extended use of de Certeau's notion of "poaching" to characterize fan writing behavior in his *Textual Poachers*.

⁷⁶Margaret Garrett has reminded me that there are other important reasons besides dissatisfaction with zine publishing for the fans' preference for circulating *Professionals* stories in a less formal way. The writing of *Professionals* fan fiction began in England where it is much more difficult than in the U.S. to produce slash fiction discreetly. Most British fans do not have the same access to self-service copiers and certainly cannot afford to have their own copy machine, as several of the U.S. slash editors do. *Professionals* stories, thus, were usually circulated in carbon copies, and only made it into Xerox form once they were sent to fans in the U.S. The "circuit" started as a way to disseminate the unpublished British stories in this country. As the *Professionals* reading audience has grown, by leaps and bounds, both in North America and Australia, these stories are increasingly being published in zines by American fans with their cheaper technology. Fans still support the "circuit," however,

according to Garrett, for its freedom, availability, and low cost.

[77]This lack of explicitness is here, however, given a fictional motivation: the information in the manual, which was accidentally transmitted during a space-warp from the *Enterprise* computer to a computer at a military installation in Omaha, Nebraska, is incomplete; Star Fleet Command has deleted any technology not known to twentieth-century Earth technology, in order to preserve the Prime Directive's dictum of nonintervention in other cultures, including the culture of the Federation's own past.

[78]See the introduction to Jenkins's *Textual Poachers* for an overview of how fans are typically characterized by both academic and journalistic writers.

[79]Kirk's thoughts, in Syn Ferguson's epic slash novel, *Courts of Honor* (1985).

[80]Constance Penley and Andrew Ross, "Cyborgs at Large: Interview with Donna Haraway," in *Technoculture*, ed. Constance Penley and Andrew Ross (Minneapolis: University of Minnesota Press, 1991), p. 18.

[81]In "Pornography by Women," Joanna Russ points out the fans' tendency to heterosexualize Kirk and Spock's sexual practices (83). In my essay "Feminism, Psychoanalysis, and the Study of Popular Culture," I try to say why many slash fans want Kirk and Spock to be, however improbably, heterosexual.

[82]Nina Auerbach, *Communities of Women* (Cambridge, Mass.: Harvard University Press, 1978).

[83]Carroll Smith-Rosenberg, "The Female World of Love and Ritual: Relations between Women in Nineteenth Century America," *Signs: Journal of Women in Culture and Society* 1 (Autumn 1975): 1-29.

[84]Nina Baym, *Women's Fiction: A Guide to Novels by and about Women in America, 1820-1870* (Ithaca: Cornell University Press, 1978).

[85]Lynn Spigel, "From Domestic Space to Outer Space: The 1960s Fantastic Family Sit-Com," in *Close Encounters: Film, Feminism, and Science Fiction*, ed. Constance Penley, Elisabeth Lyon, Lynn Spigel, and Janet

Bergstrom (Minneapolis: University of Minnesota Press, 1991), pp. 205-206.

[86]Jane Tompkins, *Sensational Designs: The Cultural Work of American Fiction, 1790-1860* (New York: Oxford University Press, 1985).

[87]Leslie Fiedler, "Home as Heaven, Home as Hell," in *What Was Literature? Class Culture and Mass Society* (New York: Simon and Schuster, 1982). My citation of Leslie Fiedler might seem a little dated because so many scholars of American literature have gone over this ground so extensively since Fiedler first argued the centrality to American literature of the mythos of interethnic male bonding. And certainly scholars have gone beyond Fiedler's personal epiphany that the domestic novels weren't "trash" but culturally significant works of American literature; this insight is now taken for granted. But Fiedler did it first, did it well, and recognized that Kirk and Spock, too, were "queer as three dollar bills," so I give him his due here.

[88]Such obscuring of the issue of race and racism in America is prevalent in both regular *Star Trek* and slash fan culture. For example, when *CCSTSG Enterprises*, a *Star Trek* fan newsletter, conducted the widest survey yet of *Star Trek* fan characteristics and attitudes—asking every imaginable demographic, vocational, and social attitude question—the category of race and any questions about racism simply did not appear. When I asked the survey organizer why issues of race and racism had not been included, he said it had never occurred to him. Daniel Bernardi's forthcoming book, *The Wrath of Whiteness: Race in Star Trek* (new Brunswick, N.J.:Rutgers University Press), is an extremely useful overview of how the issue of race has been played out in thirty years of *Star Trek*.

[89]Christopher Newfield, "Democracy and Male Homoeroticism," *Yale Journal of Criticism* 6, no. 2 (1993): 29-62.

[90]Joseph Allen Boone, *Tradition Counter Tradition: Love and the Form of Fiction* (Chicago: University of Chicago Press, 1987).

[91]Lynn Hunt, ed., *The Invention of Pornography: Obscenity and the Origins of Modernity, 1500-1800* (New York: Zone Books, 1993).

ACKNOWLEDGMENTS

I hope that my book honors the memory of popular scientist Jim Pomeroy; I wrote it in his spirit and from his example.

Andrew Ross, Paula Treichler, and Lisa Cartwright have been trusty co-PI's on several popular science experiments whose discoveries led directly to *NASA/TREK* — most notably *Technoculture* (1991) and two special issues of *Camera Obscura* on "Imaging Technologies/Inscribing Science" (1992).

I thank my very closest readers, Avery Gordon and Christopher Newfield.

Allan Langdale also gave loving attention to the manuscript.

I am more grateful than I can say to the undergraduates whose cheap labor has underpinned this whole project (at least I fed them from time to time): Thomas Csicsman, Jennifer Gimblin, Jennifer Borenstein, and especially Valeska Ramet, Keith Johnston, Jennifer Westfall, and Jamie Gluck. Thanks also to Jay Stemmle.

Those who have given me crucial advice, research gems, priceless images, or other lifesaving help include Gary Laderman,

Murray Forman, Lynn Spigel, Deborah Stucker, Stephanie Nelson, Paul Abramson, Hal Penley, Nick Chapman, Steve Fagin, Ian Balfour, Sarah Higley, Samuel R. Delany, Chris Marker, Teresa Espana, Eric White, Jeff Gunderson, Valerie Hartouni, Alexander Doty, Tamar Gordon, Mary Beth Haralovich, Ken Wissoker, Laura Grindstaff, Rachel Adams, Lawrence Badash, John Cloud, Jai Mitchell, Renée Green, and Mitchell Duneier. So many people showed me such extraodinary generosity in the course of this project that I am sure that I have forgotten to name all of them—sorry if I missed you.

The *Camera Obscura* editors deserve thanks for putting up with (and even encouraging) some of my wilder research tangents: Julie D'Acci, Elisabeth Lyon, Sasha Torres, and Sharon Willis.

I received unexpected help and encouragement from UC-Santa Barbara Chancellor Henry Yang, the former Neil A. Armstrong Professor of Aerospace Engineering at Purdue University and NASA consultant. The librarians at NASA headquarters in Washington and the photo archivists at the Johnson Space Center also gave me important (and speedy) help.

My fellow fellows in the Cornell University Society for the Humanities infamous "Mass Culture" year offered much inspiration: Alexander Doty, Rachel Bowlby, Jane Feuer, Laura Mulvey, Simon Frith, Trinh T. Minh-ha, William Gibson, Karal Ann Marling, and Thomas Ross.

Special thanks go to Margaret Garrett, Lily Fulford, Barbara Tennison, Joan Martin, Christine Logsdon, Jennifer Holland, Sharon Decker, Lois Welling, Linda Brandt, Della Van Hise, Shoshanna Green, Sandy Hereld, Sammi McGlasson, Pat

Diggs, Gayle Feyrer, Nancy Bannister, Kim Bannister, the kinky Scottish nanny, Lynn Maners, Henry Jenkins, Cynthia Jenkins, Kandy Fong, and Kathleen Resch.

The Film Studies staff at the University of California-Santa Barbara gave me much practical help; I also thank them for their enthusiasm and sense of humor: Kathy Carnahan, Marti Mangan, and Joe Palladino.

I am grateful to Verso's Colin Robinson for his patience and perseverance (good qualities in an editor). Brian Wallis did a bang-up editing job.

I have had wonderfully receptive audiences for the ideas and arguments in *NASA/TREK*. The best suggestions and criticisms have come from audiences at: Jet Propulsion Laboratory, CalTech; Institute for Contemporary Arts (London); University of Illinois at Urbana-Champaign Cultural Studies Conference; the University of Rochester Susan B. Anthony Center; Harvard University Center for Literary Theory and Cultural Studies; Princeton University J. Edgar Farnum Lecture Series; University of Alberta Dean's Inaugural Lecture Series; Whitney Museum of American Art Independent Study Program; Columbia University Film Seminar; Public Access, Toronto; UC-San Diego and the La Jolla Museum; Conference on Feminism and the Theory of the Subject, UCLA; Cornell University Society for the Humanities; Console-ing Passions Conference on Television, Video, Feminism; American Anthropology Association panel on cyborg anthropology; Stockholm Film Festival Conference on Cinema and Technology; CalArts; Wesleyan University Society for the Humanities; Wexner Center for the Arts; Universities of Warsaw, Lodz, and Cracow (Jagellonica); Autumn Film School, Ljubljana; UC-Humanities Research Institute Residency Group on "Postdisciplinary Approaches to the Technosciences"; New Museum; seminars at Queen's University Visiting Women's Scholars Program; Simon Fraser University Summer Institute for the Arts; University of Kansas Alice F. Holmes Summer Institute for Literature; and from students in my courses on "Science Fiction Film," "Theories of Popular Culture," "Modern Sex and Modern Love" (with Christopher Newfield), "Women as Producers and Consumers of Culture," "Pornographic Film," and "Freud for Beginners."

INDEX